Follow the Clear River Down

Other Books by Rob Ganson and Long Lake Press

Float Like a Butterfly
  Sing Like a Tree

L   N   L   K   P   E   S
   O   G   A   E   R   S

74705 Johannah rd.
Washburn Wi 54891
robostang@yahoo.com

Follow the Clear River Down

By Rob Ganson

Forward, by Marc Creamore

THE BEST KEPT SECRET WRITING IN AMERICA TODAY

I was introduced to Rob Ganson's work a couple of years ago while reading his first volume of poetry "Float Like A Butterfly, Sing Like A Tree" Within its pages I recognized a poet who is a descendent of Walt Whitman, a cousin of Allen Ginsberg and a new found relative to my own musings. This, his second volume of verse carries the torch of truth seeker and unabashed freedom fighter for the weary, the downtrodden and the sensitive even further. Listen as he stands on some crumbling rooftop and shouts out a warning to those who have lobotomized the hearts and minds of the general populace:

> "Oh, souless seed of man, unholy war
> that seethes through history like a pox
> and lends young men to unholy chores,
> desist in fitting young to flag-draped box."

Listen as he holds weary discourse with the soothsayers of racism and bigotry:

> "The fires of commerce consume
> aboriginal wisdom with teeth
> mislabeled Jesus, mix the ashes
> of the dead languages of actual earth
> in concrete cauldrons of
> fictional history to fill
> libraries and graves."

And listen once again as he addresses the ungodly malaise perpetrated in the name of an artificial spirituality that is only there to further the futile governing body of supposed religiosity and political pabulum:

> "With swords and napalm, they preach
> to pagans of peace and commerce,
> growing maps, multiple births that
> deny the sacred shape of womb,
> and a violent collective box, but
> these are not my boxes, that
> judge the tribes with guns
> and angry prophets."

Ah, but Rob Ganson also has the ability to delicately touch the nerves of those who are sensitive enough to recognize human tenderness and frailty. This from "Saving Grace":

"Grace was invisible to commuters and other
miscreants, but the poet saw her shining
like new money in a beggar's hand, or
rain to end the pain of drought."

And this from his poem "Mae"

> "I helped Mae lift her man
> those last few years
> and she helped me
> find one
> inside."

He is also acutely aware of the necessary need of the poet's voice in today's rather mundane and numb minded society. He holds his voice and the voices of other poets in high regard and urges them to speak freely and clearly through the fog of this sorry old world.

"A poet's rhymes should raise the reader's eye
to the stars.
Words must try, at times to shine like those
diamonds, glittering in the vast mystery.
The hands of the poet must not grasp at weapons
but tend to gardens of the mind as if to
hold the weight of the holy breast in gentler grip
and drip phrases with the rhythm of
waterfalls to salve the wounds
and lead the way, all the way, home."

Yes, the poet's voice . . . and in your hands you are holding a book of unfathomable richness, a book that will be savored by many, many generations to come. I have often thought of Rob as the best kept secret writing in America today, but I am certain that this will all change as time moves forward. His ability to turn a phrase, an image that lingers in the mind long after it's read, will become poetic manna for the children and grandchildren of future generations.

So take heed of this Wisconsin wordsmith and allow his words to coat your tongue, your heart, your mind with the raw flavor of Whitman's earthly reverence. Feel the bombs of dissatisfaction exploding inside his chest and be touched by the river of humanity that flows through his undaunted spirit.

Over the years I have grown so weary of trying to find a poetry that speaks directly to me . . . too many hours scouring dusty bookstores and vacant libraries and not finding anything to soothe and inflame my inner be-ing. Finally I have found a poet who blasts through the academic, insipid walls of language and screams and whispers neo beat psalms into my brain.

May he continue to do so, because I and many others are richer in his presence.

Marc Creamore

Marc Creamore resides in Vancouver , British Columbia and has been writing poetry for over 40 years. His published work includes 5 titles, the latest being "Notes From The Abandoned Orchard Of The Moon". Beat poetry and the musings of the ancient Asians have been important influences on his life, as well as his contemporaries, Wanda Lea Brayton, Nicolette van der Walt and the author of the book you are holding.

Contents

From the great divide, the Sioux River flows,
as clear as a babe's first innocent dream.
It seems that everything I need to know
was learned knee-deep, in this clear running stream.

I, born in a salty estuary,
more than mere fisherman, wetting a line,
am kin to the gnome, the bashful fairy,
part and parcel of mother's grand design.

The ocean, it seems is the finish line,
as man follows the clear river down,
but merchants with poisons, seeping from mines
have painted the lower river with brown.

I, with few options and little renown
paint verses to follow the clear river down.

The Faces of Joy

Joy is like dewdrops on a spider web
ignited by one more dawn;
a jubilant jester, seen
in laughing children,
and daydreams

I saw it smile once in church, but
more often on the dance floor
and seldom in eyes that judge

You can find it dancing
with a child

Salt and warm birthdays
anger, hiding

sting rays with the ace
of spades in the spokes
behind the drums
where America
ain't

"CAR!"

oak limbs, reaching
into sky-high thighs

shy

"It's over, I don't have to go!"

Frisbees, dogs in bandanas

"FREE THE BREASTS!"

Oh, yes indeed!
IT IS HER, SHE IS IT

Bohemian and so color

Nope, thump, scream

Forest, stream, she, they

Birth

A red Harley, fat, thunder
on the river

she lubes so easy, starts so
easy

Oh, Shit! Ow... repeat

It's all so beautiful
at the peak

"It's not all pork-fat
and wine, you know, not
all puppies and popcorn"

slower, and slower

voices in the forest, the

river

I hear them now, writing
rainbows, wars, orgasm,
and me

God is hiding
in me...

Ripples

{Zen # -1}

I am a salty sort of pond, buoyant
I absorb the pebble
and radiate ripples
from yesterday to tomorrow

but this poem is not about the pond,
the pebble -
and I have no time
in an empty jar.

The ravens fly, hungry
in the cold hiss of winter
and missing the kisses,
the writhing, the tithing of
glimpses beneath a brittle shell,

I squirm in the shadow of love.

The light; it won't find me
and the darkness won't hide me.
Distant coyotes sing my song.
Tried by moon, sentenced by stars,
the night, itself, finds me guilty

as I squirm in the shadows of love.
The wind remembers her laugh
and I see her eyes in the stars
while the owl asks who she was.
The sun dies, extinguished in
black velvet gloves of midnight,

and I squirm in the shadows of love.

Winter pecks at brittle bones,
my memories of hearth and home,
as even her face recedes.
The vultures circle above
a man who fingers a piece of lace

while I squirm in a shadow of love

New love wore gaudy colors.
It was all rodeo sex and picnics,
all waxing eloquent
in a blue cloud of metaphysics
and waning supine.
The gales of November would wait,
the thrown pots, the make up sex,
the weight of winter's guilt,
those words we can't
unspeak.
Laughter rang like wind-chimes.
Time stood still when eyes
sought embrace of eyes
as thighs scissored
as if friction were holy.
She wore afternoon's sun barefoot
and the stars were her tiara.
There would be time
for the light to fade,
the passion,
but for now, it was all
so very orange.

Channeling Dylan on a Monday morning in America

A farmer's hands in simple soil
will raise good crops from wealthy land
an' raise the voice of man, "AMEN!", to
plans to feed the nation his callused toil.

But now the prophets smell the oil
an' north country boys are called to fight
for freedom, delight in the light of July fourth
bombs an' come home broken or boxed.
But Grandpa fought in Viet Nam,
got slammed by the landmine, lost that foot,
put his doubts aside and stumped through
the woods for twenty years.
We always bake a ham when a hero returns
with a chestfull of ribbons and nightmares
an' welcome him home to the land where
peace replaces tears in tired eyes with

rainbows.

Grandma would've been different
but Grandpa Billy ate his ham, and went
to see Sally who'd taken up with the Judge's
son in college but then he met granny.

Jimmy, from down at the mill had died
on some rainforest hill the communists wanted
so she run off to the farm to milk the cows
an' raise strong children with love.

She cried when they made daddy a hero -
over there, where somebody set the oil on fire
an' there wouldn't be enough zeros in Texas
banks so daddy died for freedom.
Over at the mines, the iron ore feeds
the war machine that gnashes steel teeth
while the girls at the bowlin' alley bat their
lashes at the boys in the uniforms, the
soldiers.

Another wizard, behind a Washington
curtain is hungry for rural boys to lead the
way to another sandy war and even the score
with terrorists who ain't there 'till we make 'em.

I only want to work the gracious land,
to raise a garden, line our life with mason
jars on wealthy shelves, chickens cluckin',

and children, racin' the wind with kites.
My hands, so proud to hold a plow, a hoe,
a smiling wife, resist the call to hold a weapon
high an' take the life of some politician's
enemy that called his daddy names.

Grandpa says my daddy calls me there
as an heir to American glory, to give my all
to stall the tide of falling planes and rising
taxes and defend my family's
freedom.

I wanna sit on the porch an' play happy songs
'till long summer nights echo with music
and sighs, watch the red clay sprout corn
and see the light shine in her eyes.

I wanna recycle an' recirculate, abate the
greed that feeds on mother nature's broken body
to grace the face of the morning with simple
psalms, spoken by a man devoid of dogma.

Heavy horses an' good honest sweat, creaking
leather an' fresh turned earth, the mirth of
fiddlers an' children 'round the maypole,
and fingers shellin' beans know glory too.

Grandpa knows, and Granny too; now that
Johnny went to Iraq and came back in that box
it's time to leave my flock and honor his
memory by taking up arms for
America

Remember me darlin' when you go down
to the crick. Remember the picnic an' kisses.
Remember the heart that misses you in a
savage mist of blood an' torn ground.

Remember me in the gifts of the land,
the touch of my hand, the smiles of our son
when he plants new seed in the garden we grew
in the sun of too few summers.

Tell him to stay home when the dragons play,

to break the chain of bombs and grief with
a strong hand to hold love safe and deny
the thief that would bind him to glory.

There's a place in the corner of the field
where we watched we watched that sunset;
remember? Where the owl sings from the big oak
while cicadas drone the moon aloft.

Plant me there without a preacher's mirror
to hide me from the good earth. Leave one
fieldstone on top of my mound to sound
one word, painted to release my son-

peace…

Absent Grail

What quest would quench my need for meaning,
what vision, when my mirror is empty of gods,
what noble task, for a poet with leftward leanings?

 Though odd and thoughtful, prone to lofty goals,
I follow no ancient copy of my face to crusades
that seek to enslave the innocent pagan soul,
and rebuke those lords with gold and dark brigades.

Do no harm. Is that the only valid test of man?
My only weapon, this strident voice must shout
to fan the flames of peace across a once great land,
absent any god, yet loud in great cause, devout.

 The holy ghost I seek is only seen as wisps
of smoke in stormy skies, or distant thunder,
the nectar of life, sipped from the softest lips
of an earthbound angel, the wonder of love.

My eyes are only large enough for curve of earth,
too small to name a god's benevolent girth,
but large enough to set my sights above
the horizon of ambition to unearth
a reverent tear at the magic of love

It was like a song; a punk-rock song. I was watering a garden near little
boxes, wearing this, like, babies high-chair-tabletop, strapped 'round
my waist with a crunchy treat and an adult beverage; sort of post
Husker Du and colorful, but very Amerikan Sunday like plastic
flamingos, but angry, like Evil beaver or capitalism.

This bloated moment hung like a cotton-candy cloud in a sky devoid of
angels or imaginary heavens in a region of forboding conformity and
comic book breast-implants, silicone, silicon, loud commercials with no
programs and an oily green agenda –

G
   A
B
B
   A

G
   A
B
B
   A

 In chunky plastic bass-notes; fast and wrong, like a potted-palm on a
skateboard with a voice like fingernails, shredding the daily paper,
screaming against wars into air that ain't dead yet, but oily, like
Vaseline on a lens in the best punk-rock song I seen in my whole-born-
daze, and it's all real because my beard itches.

{for Walt Whitman}

i could not fly
until i knew my arms were not wings
couldn't walk
until i had nowhere to go
i am not mirror-bound
to function
but spirit clothed

we could not dance as lovers
until our albatross
was healed in the light
of such poesy
as wolfsong, poured from the moon

our children are not sprung
from writhing eel
or single-blooded womb
but by the excrement
of stars

they will seep down many rivers
waft on the breath of earth
by the grace of magic
i cannot name
but feel

{for ol' Buk}

I was drunk on her sex.
Just a whiff, and I was flopping
like a carp, gasping.
Right away she wants me
to buy her things,
says, remember how I
pulled her hair,
drinking while I
pounded away, how I
shocked her
with that cold beer
on her back,
says,
that should be worth something,
daddy.

When the beer was gone,
the booze, the job,
the rent money,
her eyes didn't look for me
like they did.
The moaning stopped,
and finally, the humping.
While I was drinking my
last dollar
she took everything
I never had
and left.

The big bum on the corner
had an attitude,
and then, a bloody nose.

Bitch!

I looked for god in mirrors and dreams,
in churches, in temples,
in rivers and streams.

Her name remained silent to my ears
and her countenance
remained dim.

I looked in books full of fables
and legends of saviors
who look like me

but the books were all too heavy;
the pastors preached for war
their gods only wanted more.

I speak of myself with a lower case i
when I see her in the sky, see
children with shining eyes
and finally relax

about questions
of why.

From magic womb, born of tides
and by false gods consumed
we fail to hear the drums
and feet forget
to dance

We chance upon metronomes
of days that fade to missions
of endless buffoonery
on conveyor belts
in boxes

Some of us, the poet, the painter
the seekers of distant star
hear again, the drum
from afar, stir our
silent feet

to greet the morning with silent song, and
raise our eyes from task to sky, to
join the tribes in one more dance
and teach our children
to fly

The box there was gift wrapped
with numbers upon it
Two thousand and nine
was spelled out on the tag
It contained plastic soldiers
with bright little flags
The children's bright faces
were lit by hope's magic
but all the king's warlords
with tragic agendas
were seeking dark glory
while peace was forsaken
and children were broken
as orders were issued
to tear at their tissues
in the language of saints

The lands were all painted
with rivers of crimson
War is no game
for the fickle or faint
The dungeons of Texans
resound with the screaming
of men who are broken
for speaking the truth
against the dark warlords
well armed, and uncouth

Across the bright oceans
the bombs are still bursting
to paint all new borders
on those distant lands
Some fight for Allah
and some fight for Jesus
but all of the heroes
spill blood on the sands

Africa's burning
with murderous rampage
as children are watching
their mothers are raped
Monsters are sated
and nations created
The cameras are rolling
It's all being taped
Kings are elated
and hungers abated
by victims, all bleeding
for the soldiers they lead
Many are taken
but few have escaped.

II

They promise us changes
but old men are greedy
and blind to the needy
The media hides them
in celluloid falsehoods, but
leaders don't read Braille
Technology brings corrupt
squires erections
while helpless and homeless
don't drink from the grail

The gulf between wealthy
successful and healthy
and the drones that
supply them with homes
and food, dumped into
an ocean of shame
just grows, but we know
it's so fucking wrong
and we go along
just the same

The game is still fixed
by the by the rich man that sits

on the throne, atop the hill
while the meek in the valley
are tortured and killed
The knights of dark realms
are sent to the slaughter
the sons and the daughters
of lower caste mothers
by the monsters at the helm

WE, the proud others
the sisters and brothers
that preach revolution
are silenced by powers
that seek to extinguish
the voices of hope
They hid evolution
behind heavy bibles
that fall on our women
with second-class shame
They hide gentle Jesus
and colonize nations
in his mispronounced name
enslaving young men
to the horrors of war
by promising glory
with fables about
fortune and fame

III

Our mother is dying
and the do-gooders sigh
as if we can't stop the beast
Our umbilicus is kinked
We're dying quite slowly
If the preachers and kings
we continue to follow
sink polar icecaps
in oceans of poison
our sons and our daughters
will soon be extinct
The polar bears sink

while first ladies sport mink
from behind the powdered
masks of ancient whores
The stars are invisible
in the land, indivisible
by mercy or justice
by shame in the mirrors
of cogs in the heavy wheel
that seal mother's doom
with refusal to heal
The smog that consumes
cities, devoid of pity
for men, who've gone astray
while disaster looms, and
all we can do is raise
blinded eyes to pray

Cancer is chewing away
at our farmland
The genie's been released
and the monster's at play
on the flesh of our mother
that fortune has flayed
to exhibit her treasures
in earth's dying days
We've taken our pleasuses
with rabbit mathematics
as if procreation were
God's greedy plan
Our rivers are salted
with profit's dank stain
as the sky weeps tears
of increasingly acid rain

We troubadours, sharing
our fear and our caring
for creatures, run amuk
must shout truths, enlightened
to nations of frightened
victims of war, proclaim
a new age, a turning of pages
an opening of eyes
The sky holds the secrets
of prophets and sages

obscured by the soot
of petroleum cages
patrolling the land
that our hands have so torn
with commerce, born of greed
It isn't too late to reverse fate
and close the gates of hell
and plant the seeds of peace

IIII

Our voices are weapons
with lessons of nature
to raise delinquent alarms
Elated, we sing the praises
of farmers, who raise the corn
We write newer fables
that grace dinner tables
with talk of simple things
as the millennium of waste
is shorn from future history
as a cleaner age is born
Our votes, our refusal
to be used as mere fodder
for the gods of war
our retreat from consumption
could still clear the rivers
and open the sky to birds
The stars may still twinkle
and freedom's bells tinkle
if our brothers grasp a clue
The crops could still flourish
with grains that nourish
the children of the sun
A new day is breaking
for children forsaking
the dynamo of greed
as dollars are falling from grace
Release us from vultures
adorned with dark power
The time for change is here
The hour is now

to take up the plow
and put our violence to rest
We have one more chance
to uproot all the monsters
and pass our ultimate test
to unite the brotherhood of man
to a green new plan
to unite our divided flocks
and coerce Pandora
back into her box

Unwound

She is discarded in porcelain repose,
as if the new cuddle could so warm
as a forgotten lover's touch, at rest
in a box of pain.

Streaked mascara is worn within
as if a faint grin could reclaim
that part of her, so broken
by those angry words he spoke,
three tokes to the wind
and hungry for new flesh.

She waits with the other
discarded toys, motionless,
her soundless grief, profound,
as if her spring had
come unwound.

{for Carl Sagan and Moby}

I am not the walrus
   but star stuff, you see
like the earth beneath my feet

There is no Cadillac constellation
   and Orion does not hunt
men

The neon church is ours
   to explore

but we fashion mirror gods
   to sponsor our wars

We know mother is carbon based
   but we fill her breath
   with burning blood

and her song is laced
   with death

The big dipper is filled with water
   but our blasphemies poison
our rivers

Apathetic eyes don't seek the sun
   and the air is growing
   hotter

We are all made of stars, you see
   the birds, the bees
   the soil, the trees

We anoint ourselves the kings of these
   and tip our circle

with the vast fruit
of our wombs

burn the blood of ancients
while disaster looms

All that glitters is gold, indeed
if found in the midnight sky

yet our hungry eyes are full
of ourselves

blind to the light that feeds
our need for mystery

We fill our history with the blight
of war

genocide to identify the virus
that turns day to night
with sacred ash

I threw a pebble
a grain of mother earth
into a pond
alive with countless stars

The ripples painted a universe
of circles

that spread from my feet
to mars

with a reverent sigh
with a tear in my eye

I found my church

in the very sky

The night tasted like wet dog and diesel. Even the neon was gray.
Vignettes of mayhem and endings had begun with a quick one
with the boys, after the whistle blew open the gates of steel. The ol'
lady had been on another fucking rampage over bills, broken promises,
those panties in the glove box.

"Fuck you!" "No, Fuck you!" My Harley knew the way back to the bar.
The beers gave way to the corn, pride of Tennessee and , well, we
got a bit rowdy. Doris got pretty interesting as we bought back and
forth, so of course, I was sitting with her when the ol' lady showed
up. After she was gone, {for good, this time} I celebrated with a
bathroom blowjob from Doris.

The redneck came in around one-thirty. I had about half-a-monster
on to trump his two beers and strong opinions about long hair and
black leather. He was still talkin' when fightin' time came. I missed
a little. Oh, his nose was broke, but I laid my god damn eyebrow
open. I had to fire down a couple before Doris taped it shut in the
John.

I tipped the scooter on the way to the after party; wrecked about
five hundred bucks worth of chrome, not to mention Doris' dress.
Some soldier had brought home a bunch'a opium. I didn't know the
pool was empty, and I think I broke a couple'a ribs. The fog fucked
with the ignition all the way back to the apartment, strewn with all my
scissored clothes. It was Saturday night, and I knew my mouth would
taste like ass come Sunday.

in your fresh and ancient frame,
holy in your kinship as goddess.

Whip-thin or robust, the poetry of man
is tested with the angle and flesh of you,
healed in the clasp to your breast.

You carry the minstrel of the moon,
the quiet thunder of tides
in hips that dance
for me.

Never mind the fun-house-mirror
of glamour, fashion's narrow view;
you are hewn from magic,
a prestadigater, a song
come to life.

The balm of sight is available
to my eye, the lotion I apply to woman
is but a rhyme to paint on parchment's
face, to grace the arms that hold me near,
a soul that knows the way to Xanadu.

I lusted after the girl, loved the woman,
but I worship the crone...

On Turning Black

A pale hippy, I walked the black streets
looking for the blues.
Lightning struck, and making friends
by Braille, I ran amuck to
accommodating rhythms.
Oh, there were straight razors
and militant Muslims
but the rainbow gentled
with love, paisley
an a wooly booger
doin' the albino boogie
grew cotton in his bones.
They called me the nappy-headed-white-boy.

The Homeless Woman Koan

 She pushed a shopping cart down State Street
talking to people that weren't but
they were wrong anyway, for
doing her like that.
Her cat wore a sweater. She wore
twenty-three or some other magic number of cotton ~
of wool colors, blended by the city to gray.
Now, I hadn't prayed in quite some time
but SOMEONEs god oooohmed in my head.
The empty wallet and the sense that I was the
gifted one, led to the yellow brick road to fortune
and hushed stories of love, bruises
and the nervous hospital replaced the concert.
The blond that picked me up, hitchin' on 80
tasted like hope.

Fetus

I never knew him, or of him
until she wanted to hurt me, you see
to slide that imagined knife deep
between ribs to the heart of me.

THUMP!
I hear it in my darkest nights
in the back alleys of my own construction
written in blood on angry testosterone streets
in the thick wet fog that only adjectives
paint with nearly opaque intentions.
I hear it when I pass the dumpsters
just that THUMP, and a thin cry
to help me die   a little.

When the Lights Bent

When the lights bent, the city
was a circus tent with eight clowns.
Gliding from the ballroom to the rocks
to pick up a page from Dr, Leary's book.
I was hooked, on the leash of the beast.
A multicolored dynamo in my head
led to the greener pastures
of beatniks and day glow daisies
on paisley busses that went even further
than the maps in my interior kaleidoscope.
The city glowed like lunar rainbows
and there were still blonds.

Goin' to the Country

I rode my horse into the bars
but the horse rode me out.
"CUT YER FUKIN' HAIR!" they hollered from
pickups with Skynyrd stickers, before
the ultraviolence ensued.
Battered and bruised, even though
LSD25 trumps MAD DOG 20-20
in the event of fisticuffs, I was swollen
and broken. Cut to the quick by a blond
I threw a pebble into a pond.
As I was weaving on the south edge
of the pond, the ripples spread north
to a land of clearer waters.
My car chased the north star
to another blond.

If my middle finger ever wore shoes
I believe it would sport hob-nailed boots.
I'd throw them at the guy on evening's news,
the one with the grin that the truth disputes.

If I ever met Dubya on the street,
that usurper of trusting young men,
I'd pummel him with the soul of both feet
pick up those two boots and fling them again.

That greedy Texan lied to start a war,
tortured the meek, stained the name of my land,
and fed the wealthy by starving the poor.
Salute him with a middle fingered hand!

All hat and no cattle, that's our leader
a lying moron; a bottom feeder –

good riddance, asshole...

Carnival I - Lights

Above the quaking corn and tiny town
glow the lights of carnival, sparkling like
rainbows, jovial as the dancing clown,
energized by laughter of little tykes.
Never mind the carnies and their blank stares,
Laugh and scream; eat the greasy food and dream.
This is the place to leave behind your cares,
where magic is cheap, nothing as it seems.

Win your sweetheart a purple teddy bear,
and steal a kiss amongst the neon lights.
Celebrate a Midwestern county fair,
quake with giddy glee, and shudder in fright.

Bend yourself odd in the funhouse mirror.
The freaks in the sideshow see you clearer.

Neon lights assault the prairie burg
It's Saturday night in the rural landscape
and the carnival has come to town

We, the tattooed hordes,
the outcasts of the united conformity
have crafted a magic world of light
of delight and fright
of twisted nocturnal might ~
have taken over this Midwestern
summer night

and you are invited

See yourself as we
in the funhouse mirror
twisted and deformed; see what it's like
when you don't conform
to uncle Sam's grand design

" STEP RIGHT UP, SEE THE MONKEY BOY"
    he barks, "SEE NATASHA DANCE"

Sweaty hands rustle in daddy's pocket

In the shadows, I read the insecure cheerleader
by moist Braille, chew on fear
with a predatory radar
for the meekest sheep to fleece

With my cotton candy wig
and greasepaint, my bulbous proboscis
I troll for wee fish
with big shoes and a hard lap

The tortured voices
of sorrow's menagerie roar
and trumpet the song of bars ~
the insane gibberish of the caged
while I observe the corn dog
eating country girl
with her tube-top
that stands out
as hungry for pirates, pointed
at the next bad decision

On the rides, the kiddies scream
showering the crowd with hot dogs
and used ice cream

vomit gleams on tear-streaked faces

It's all like a dream
riding on the black horse
on the merry-go-round
reaching for the last gold ring
that gleams in moist eyes
of innocence

Billy Joe won Jane a Big Teddy Bear
so he could give her a pearl necklace
away from the eyes of light

There is another carnival in the shadows
where the rainbow lights wont reach
where the professors of darkness preach
of pleasures the nuns don't teach

Where the black sheep of America graze
in the halcyon nights of summer
where the girls are naïve
and the hungry carnies prey

Welcome to the village of the lost
where we know the cost of night
on the souls of those
who forsake the light of day
to let midnight
have it's way, welcome

"STEP RIGHT UP!"

Carnival III – Becoming

{For Wanda}

I've never left the carnival, really
reaching for that golden circle
from the back of that black horse
distracted by the lights
and sweat on silk .

When I wear the big shoes
the red nose, the sad painted smile
and the fun house mirrors
have had their way with me
again

i perceive goddesses, beckoning
from the infinite neon moons

the swan, gliding with open
wings, a seat for me at night
when I'm weary or torn
shorn of self
and a downy nest
to rest a spirit
and promise new dawns

A neon iris, with an African bloom

looming when my color
has gone, pinned to my red blazer
with a pointed reminder
of beauty

My niece, the acrobat, defying gravity
daughter to a lost brother
i never met, keeper of
Eastern light, applying the lotion
of motion – retrograde emotions
festooned across my sorrow
like a quilt or soothing Koan.

These are the calliopes I hear
in my inner ear, the mistresses
of the light
who sing to me, hiding
in the shadows, behind
the freak show tent

My tattoos are stories of the road
that writhe like the contortionist
behind the gaudy curtain
naked to the gaze of citizens
that don't see themselves
in colors

i find better questions
on the midway
meatier than chanted answers
beneath revival tents
questions about the source of
these lights, the three rings
in life's vast circus

i find better questions
in the sideshow
and wear them three layers deep
in the flesh i paint
so as to avoid
scaring the tourists

The back of the long dog is hunched like a bumpy albatross
  on the road, the road, the road to enlightenment
  in a redwhiteandblue formica wasteland
  smelling of last night's waitress, smelling of tequila
  smelling of Josho's dog on wet Monday.

A knapsack reeks of poems and the asphalt Koan
  reverberates to expansion cracks on the face of America
  while erstwhile merchants scurry in the blur
  of unforeseen circumstances and capitalist mayhem
  and he shares a joint with a soldier of ill fortune.

There are nipples and other sexual propaganda cavorting
  in the background of a movie, playing on memory's screen -
  unseen scenes of writhing buffoonery sparkle in a poem
  that he probably will not write
  tomorrow.

Nevertheless, golden arches arch, parched preachers imbibe
  and Kansas is streaming live, beyond the frosted monitor.
I can not corroborate this evidence of genius' reincarnation
  but only describe him, clothed in diesel denim, smoke;
  envisioning the stanzas he chants from that lurching bus
  that bus in all of us, we denizens of the road.

He is back in all these things that sing in the last four rows
  where nocturnal missions unfold to a cadence
  of yellow dashes and the chants of inebriated saints
  and black eyed trailer wives, running, running, running
  to the next factory worker that's only mean
  when he's corned up, but he needs her, an' he's sorry.

He's in that armadillo, flat on the shoulder, spelling sorrow –
  in the driver, the guide on a metaphysical quest
  in the blank daze of the soldier, seeing himself as carrion
  in the mantra of firestone, the hum of geography
  beneath the wheels of progress
  in an imaginary greyhound
  in the back of my mind.

and a happiest new year,
Jesus, he's a comin'
I swear, it ain't a myth
I know all 'bout your daddy –
how he preyed on all your fears
I know about your lovin' Jim –
how he died in that distant paddy
but soon it'll be the twenty-fifth
an' he's comin' to dry your tears

I know you live beneath the overpass
on highway six-sixty-six
kneeling for another john
Spit the seed in the gutter
and buy an angry fix
while he commutes to the suburban
labyrinth to install baby jesus
on a carefully manicured lawn

 I know they took your babies
I know they took your soul
I know that last nights meal of
track-rabbit had the rabies
I know you've lost control
I know we don't see you, I know we're blind
The world's been lost to the business man
and there just ain't time to be kind

Santa ain't got much for you Sally –
some dried up turkey from a volunteer
before he goes home to his football and beers -
full of good will, and the same turkey -
the satisfaction of the ones who care -
the sincere few who hear you weep
while you limp back to heartache and fear
and you won't be healed by sympathetic tears
or the commuters who point and leer -
knowing there are those who shine

When will the rest see you, we cogs in the wheel
afraid to acknowledge, afraid to feel
for a woman we've lost, asleep on Jesus
birthday in a cardboard box
while we celebrate behind a squadron of locks
in the Babylon behind gates of steel

Merry Christmas Mr. Jackson

asleep beneath that dock on Venice beach
I know that peace was beyond your reach
Uncle sugar wanted another hero from the streets
and a lottery spilled out yer name
to save France from a corporate retreat
an' he sent you to the jungle
to play the devil's game

 I know all about Monsanto, and Operation Ranch Hand –
about the orange that twisted your only son
I know about the horse you rode, the quiet's dark command
and the way that morpheus drowned out the sound of guns
I know the fuckin' VA cut you loose, without a dollar or hope
when nothing would stop the panic except a twenty bag of dope

I know about your sculptures, the carefully piled rocks –
the way they knock them down each night to mock
the gentlest man on the boardwalk, with peace to preach
to all who'll listen to the prophet who lives beneath the dock
a man who loves a god he can't quite reach

 I know about the boys that your monoliths portray
and the wasted lives the fallen represent
I know the hearts of the society have gone badly astray
We are blind and our national psyche is badly bent
When their monuments are knocked down every day

But still, you smile and wish me peace
with eyes that shine like diamonds
to remind me of the value of the least
and my seat at the feast
of unexpected saints

I am a universal soldier in the lost battalion of the sighted –
in the corps of those loud few who swing the sword
of words in a peaceful war of stanza and verse to curse the blind
and remind the weary traveler on the way to holy Wal-Mart
that a conscience may be bought for the paltry sum of $20.00
at the nearest homeless shelter, "WHAT A DEAL!"
" WHAT A STEAL!" and while yer at it, seal the deal
with a smile, a kindly word for the people at the feet
of the great society

I'm a wordslinger of some small and meek renown,
that rides into a coffee shop, a theatre, on a steed of words –
crowds the mic with larger, louder adjective ~ accusatory noun
to preach to the herd of competent consumers, spread the news
of the invisible woman, the hungry man, burrowing in their
garbage cans to find their daily bread, expand their views
to include the people that America forgot

 Because I'm that homeless man, you're that homeless hag
burrowing in the shopping bag that contains all her worldly goods
but for that corporation, beneath that unfurled flag, that symbol
of freedom and glory that overlooks the banks, best give thanks
for the paychecks that keep us from being them or them
from breeching the gates of suburbia from the alley or the slum
for the sum of our difference is but numbered wisps of paper –
transient as the winds of change

You see, we are they, and they are we, some, the spent artillery
that bought your freedom, or them that fell on the fields of love
Some, the victims of the distillery, some imagine angels above
the horde of blind cogs on the wheels of so-called progress
Some of you worship, some of you pray on the day of his birth
but remember the gentle Jesus when your eyes are drawn away
from the dirty ones who've lost the way to the road to success
Offer a smile, and a seat at your table, start a new and hopeful
fable about a land where the richest remember the least
with an invitation to the Christmas feast, a new day, beneath
a universal Christmas tree, where we all have a ticket

Love is indigenous

    to the geography of the human heart

Sometimes Beauty is the pathway

    by which it travels

I found you a wee flute

    with butterflies and hummingbirds

    in it's little voice

The man who coaxed it from a tree

    infused it with these

Your grandpa sees them like stained-glass

    fairies, waiting on the porch

    to fly in your young eyes

    like flowers with a map to love

I'm sorry we let the monsters out to play

    with our building blocks

but your light will shine clearer than ours

    and the flowers will bring them

Grandma will tend these magic flowers

with love and gentle songs

The bees, the butterflies, will dance bright

　　on the winds of change

　　you will stir with your song

Your flute will sing with birds and northwind

　　to decorate the future with music
They will sing with your voice, your breath

　　and show you the way

　　to wonder...

I see my garden With Lewis Carroll's eyes

It's a blind pair of eyes that only see back
as if the fruit unplanted
will nourish –

yesterday will not spring from
the seeds of tomorrow.

I plant children in my garden
that if the dreary cities fall
they will read my poems
as hieroglyphics
in generations of maize.

Guilty!
Guilty as sin, Judge Anderson, Yes indeed;
Guilty as a white-robed fool at a dark barbeque
Guilty as the father of darkness and threats
    of what would happen if she told
Guilty as the mother who will not see
Guilty as a ginourmous Cadillac
Guilty as the blind man among the homeless
Guilty as a back-door priest
Guilty as Ronald Ray-Gun with a bladder
    full of wasted lives to piss down on the poor
Guilty as a silent man in a field of screams
Guilty as a father with a blood-stained belt
Guilty as the last man standing
Guilty as a predatory penis at last call
Guilty as a wealthy woman, serving out her
    conscience with volunteer work
    at the soup kitchen; all superior 'n shit
Guilty as the time I turned my back
Guilty as the janitor at planned parenthood
Guilty as a Texan with bloody hands
Guilty as a soldier
Guilty as the businessman, the lawyer
Guilty as Kent State
Guilty as a Frenchman in Viet Nam
Guilty as Monsanto
Guilty as the pilots in "Operation Ranch Hand"
Guilty as the ones that flew above Japanese islands
    with the building blocks of the universe
    flying to name me freedom
Guilty as Anne, or Sylvia, guilty as Hemmingway
Guilty as old Buc
Guilty as a virus
Guilty as that crazy hag from Alaska
Guilty as I was when I burned that fridgidare box
    that Johnny could have moved on up into
Guilty as Babylon

Guilty as the poet who writes about nothing of
   consequence
Guilty as the parent who only sees their children
   in the mirror
Guilty as the builders of dams
Guilty as the library
   that barred the gates to the big gay wolf
Guilty as the critic
Guilty as the cynic
Guilty as the Ad -Man
Guilty as Daly
   as Daumer
   as Nader
   as Ed Gein's trunk
   as Hitler
   as Bush
   as Tricky Dick
   as Slick Willie
   as Mrs. Slick Willie
   as Billy C.
   get over Billy already
   you can't be the voice of blue-collar America
   if you've never grown a callus...
Guilty as the pirate who boards the innocent ship
Guilty as the abuse of power
Guilty as the man who paints out the grafitti
Guilty as the freak who waited at the glory hole
   with a hatpin
Guilty as the bull at the cosmic railyard
Guilty as Dr. Gonzo's red convertible
Guilty as the preacher of one true lord
Guilty as the singer of angry psalms
Guilty as pale Mississippi
Guilty as Dante
Guilty as hell
Guilty as a judge
Yes, yer honor, I'm guilty;
I was drunk when I crashed that automobile
   an' I'm here for my lumps...

A sculpture holds the very soul of man
in a poem of flesh
and I, but stone, which is born of this
the third from sun
would carve clean rivers
on America's dear face.

The farmer plies the flesh of earth
with rows of food for thought
that emerge to love's most holy reigns
in the time of dancing children.

His wife, good woman, sings the moon aloft
rising like the bread in the warm
kitchen of her womb, holy
as the scriptures carved
in the library of rivers.

The red man, dancing in the forest, knows
that the circle of seasons shows
night the light that morning –
sun's bright author grows.

The poet would remit, to future's child
the laughter of water over stone,
the glorious inevitability
of a river's search for oceans,
or a lover's search for truth.

Oh, the lover, the hungry saint
that holds dear the other soul
to shine in his inner eye
like a sun-warmed fruit
to appease that most holy thirst
is most blessed of all organic
sculptures, the meat
of the beating heart
that knows the rhythms of god.

Hey Uncle Sam, you face-shootin' motherfucker
you rootin' tootin' convolutin' bringer of shame
GIMME BACK MY AMERICA!

Johnny, got his gun, went off to Viet Nam
off to the slaughter like a little lamb
I wish he may, I wish he might
find him a warm place
to sleep tonight

Johnny was a hero, Johnny was a saint
went off to fight the yellow man
with nary a complaint

Johnny came home FUBAR, nightmares riding him
but not as bad as the shock of his babies twisted limbs
when Monsanto's gift of orange
turned Johnny's whole world dim

Johnny's under the overpass, livin' in a box
with a monkey on his back
and no clean sox, just another man
pickin' his supper from a garbage can
The V. A. turned him out, you see
all his benefits spent
Johnny's just another casualty
and greed will not relent

James done got his papers, went off to Iraq to fight
while Haliburton flourished, to shareholders delight
James drove into an ambush, got his face blown off
reached up to feel it, all wet, an' soft
Even though his eyes were gone
and the medical officers scoffed
he saw the limbless children - bloody little pawns
broken in the fight

James, he grabbed a scissors, drove it in his heart
He didn't feel like a hero, so he chose

to depart
James's flag draped coffin was planted in the ground
beneath an earthen mound of ice
He'd paid the highest price
for the only job he found

Uncle Sam is hungry, hungry for your sons
He wants to make 'em soldiers
furnish them with guns
teach 'em to be colder
send home some torture pictures
an' make it look like fun
to rape and plunder
so fat white men grow richer
with lucre James has won

Uncle Sam is hungry, hungry for your dough
hungry for your hard earned cash
to make that black blood flow

Unkle Sam's a lawyer, he makes the rules
enslaving the pauper like cattle or fools
NOW WHERE'S MY FORTY ACRES?
WHERE'S MY FUCKIN' MULE?

Uncle Sam's a rich man
Uncle Sam's a thief
He trickles down on the middle class
like piss on rotten beef

It's time for the meek to rise
to claim a larger slice of pie
to refuse to kill or die
to stand united in one clear battle cry
to raise the lost battalion
like Ginsberg or Robert Bly
to shreik as one into
the free American sky
in one united voice
no longer shy, demanding -

WE'RE HERE FOR OUR FUCKING INHERITANCE!

When winter's first tongue
sticks to the metal
of my discontent
the first blue poems
spawn.

I see only ice
in these diamonds.

These varnished spumes
alight on the chain-link
that will release me
when April illuminates
the gate.

Cold

When November reigns in the forest -
festoons the cleavage
of river with jewels
and adorns the oak
with ice

We rest in our caves of piney corpse
contemplating stalactites
with diamonds of tears
streaming from the eyes
of winter.

When Kings were born of such
and God presided over screams in Spain
it was devilish men who wielded lash –
who stretched the ropes to question pain.
Such ghosts, such thin apparitions remained
that any offered truth was sung in dim refrain.

To darkest Africa, men were sent with chains –
smallpox blankets for dancers on America's plains.
They were put to the question, and one "true" god, explained.
Across the breadth of Europe, the question was put again.
Midwives were burned as goodness died and evil was ordained.
As ovens crackled, six million ceased to call god another name.

In a castle, in America, George II took on the question's reins.
Pyramids of Muslims were stacked to celebrate his reign.
God whispered in his ear as countless men and women were slain.
Many wrongs make right as a voice's status Quo is maintained.
In other lands, bombs are set, and blood spreads god's great stain,
His many names are spoken in the sound of thunder and flames.

In the sky, the rivers, I see god's face where seeds of peace are lain
and thus the psalms I sing are quiet, simple, quite mundane.
It is with gentler hands that I receive the key to god's domain.
GOD IS LOVE, and in her name, from darker questions, I refrain.
Any man with violent gods, speaks in tongues false and profane.
I look at these with terror and a sort of weeping disdain

and I only hope I've not lived such love in vain.

When words caress as if
a gentle wind has touched
the soul

or so inflame the eye that notions
are born from stanza's thigh –

when dance is born or music
formed of verbose clay –

when kings are shorn
of ambition's violence
in the blink of a well-turned
phrase –

a poem is the author
of this.

Ghost # 2

To scent that wind tossed snare
that drew me so to suckle at your breath
do I search each morning's whispers.
Though years have washed my sight of you
and earth consumed the flesh I crave,
when the roundest month brings lavender
I can still smell your hair…

When I went down
the rabbit hole
and realigned with my
good tribe

I merged an erstwhile poet's soul
and thus rebuked
the merchant's bribe.

When first I drank
a lover's kiss
and my cord was cut
 by magic,

I had no need for violent bliss
or skin to writhe
at the tragic.

 I joined the daisy battalion
with peaceful epithets

 to hurl,

riding Dr. Leary's stallion,
with the tie-dyed flag
I unfurled.

I was born empty
to this feast,

a vessel filled with room
for peace.

Pierce not my heart with spirit's dark decay,
 with kings so dim, I need no further plight.
Happiness is bright, and darkness, death at play.

A poet knows the cost we must defray
 as daytime grows infused with gnawing night,
pierce not my heart with spirit's dark decay.

The rising moon brings hope we must obey.
 As Bush recedes, a black man brings the light.
Happiness is bright, and darkness, death at play.

When shadows call, a poet must portray,
 and sing the shackles of depression's blight.
Pierce not my heart with spirit's dark decay.

It seems Armageddon is underway,
 but light is sought with all my pen's vast might.
Happiness is bright, and darkness, death at play.

Though nighttime's wars assault me with dismay,
 the sun will rise, revealing day's delight.
Pierce not my heart with spirit's dark decay,
happiness is bright, and darkness, death at play.

with the last heat of
the sun's loud drum
and the spice of summer
eroding
into the ginger of autumn's
decay.

No more the saffron days
or the bright smile
of Rosemary
splashing in the creek
where the watercress
defies frigid calendar.

The rich palette spent,
it is only this nondescript
hue that leads us
into the blue teeth
of a hungry winter.

I will wrap tight
this gingerbread man
against that night.

LP Tank

It sits in my yard
Like an iron
Suppository
Or a demanding blimp
While my mother burns
In the furnace

Call me fat Elvis
in my jumpsuit of words

that strive to be what
i cannot, luminous
or some other relevant
elevation of idea.

Call me a purveyor of
numerous adjectives, populous
bendings of silent rules

writing in angular colors,
that seek refrigerator magnets
and gold stars,

but NEVER call me Ishmael…

Dali Bent My Clock

Even the wind seems to wheeze now.
The columns of me read like failed
mathmatics.

This can not be my time, my sand
that runs so.
I have chosen my bed, but my moment
seems to overtake my assignment.

Who is that old man gasping
in my mirror?

Pastors and prophets came
    and went
    like leaves of orange,
    ochre, green.
My feet paint paisley chronicles
    on vistas behind brown eyes.
Many gems glint from crystal rivers,
    regarding gravity
    and circular time.
There will be cerulean days
    and lead,
    with breasts and poems,
    injuries that weep, like
    children or armies.

Somewhere, along the sacred river of days
    there is a bench beneath a willow -
    near a riffle, where trout paint
    the present in cobalt and chrome
    and there is no need for gods.
There may be an old and fuzzy man
    there
    with a tablet, finger cymbals,
    a joint.
Is he chanting?
Is he energizing some static verse?
If he is there, the bench will speak -

    "Wet Paint"

    and the water never stops.

Late at night, and in my cups,
I chanced along a darkened alley,
as though I heard some demon's pups,
barking from a cave in Raven's valley;
from a dumpster,
I heard a children's song erupt.

All my vultures flew home to roost.
My ears did ring like the iron bells of hell!
I thought the very hounds were loosed;
or was I dancing with some dead
and rotting belle
in a dingy rhyme from Proust?

Halloween and the spirits stirred,
in the grip of an infamous wind.
I felt myself in the grasp of thunderbird,
torn asunder by the weight of sins,
and that tiny voice I heard
from the mouth of an open bin.

It seems the dumpster's booming treatise
was the song of my only son,
the unborn fetus.

Born of womb, it is light we first see
and see; the sea from which we spring
is no mere god but that moist center
of woman
and she that drives the tides
and adorns her hair with stars
needs no flying angel
or name beyond moon.
Oh, swoon we must in mystery's eye
for it is ours to turn circle
to wheel, and steal some larger stature
to celebrate with stained glass
and tribes of coordinated gyrations
while songs of giants are sung
and skin-drums play at heartbeat
but there lacks a need for gods
to dance with stars our feet
don't know.
Just sew the seeds we must, as germination
that son of sun and water's fall
is all we really need.
We feed on
simple fare that breeds no church
yet nourishes much
and so this simple ground
will hold me deep, feed me in turn
to the germs of future's attention
and it is enough…

THERE IS A GOD IN MY BODY!

or is this just more dyslexic barking?

The waves of gain that crash against my meek host
are not carved from sheaves of wheat
but grist from some rain bowed mill
where poets write psalms
and bloody battles –
meat that would rot atop some distant hill
where prayer-flags flap
in the breath of dogs that speak in tongues -
that lap at the turgid nipple
of a complete circle
and such this must all be
or I would not.

The soil is obviously the host
and not some over-sublimed wafer
and my blood is not wine for future hippies
and my get, those progressive organisms
need no such imagined dogs
but merely to survive the great engines
we cause to obscure the tiny penis
of he who seeks the road to safer greed.

{He is the man on the corner -
Eating his own hand}

Never mind legends of old lost dogs
as such are the thin soup of the
ill-used medulla, asleep beneath a bible -
but mind you the crackling log -
keeping you warm inside
the solitary mind of an awakened
anachronism.
You may find yourself there
on a Tuesday.

{With apologies to Jack Kerouac}

"Who?" asks the swivel-headed lizard bird?
 {I do my best to answer}
 Coyote plays tricks on fox at the opera
while the rabbit screams
in soft, wet fur.
The pill bug reminds me of the circular
nature of things beneath it all.
The monarchs dance in zero gravity
on the way to Jack's Mexico.
Ursis is midnight, with blackberries
in odd reminders of his dominion.
The salmon jumps into another reality
to cross geographic barriers to orgasm
The trout will not succumb to
current events.
The dace will lose the race
and reside in the trout.
The deer seem to attract my arrows
and cars.
The fat guy with the mask
knows the way into the refuse
but seems out-of-place with hands.
The fischer is a mink from some
1955 giant animal mutant epic.
Someone stole the mink.
The loon shows off his tuxedo
while his courting flute
is carved from the aforementioned trout.
The dogs let me think I'm the master.
The women envelop my member ship
in the quiet waters of Venus.
The woodpecker is a drill.
The Bobcat thinks he is a panther
but he has the wrong ass.
The ass is in the pasture
where woodcock mine brown yogurt
for worms.
The ducks are all wet.
The hummingbirds love plastic flowers
and draft hyper offspring for the wasp wars.

The spring peepers remind us   54
that orgies are fun.
The ancient toad beneath the porch
has the Buddha spirit.
The falcon is a show-off.
The people are a parasitic fungus.
The roughest grouse plays the back-beat.
The turkeys are only giant chickens
that yodel when aroused.
The army worms are slippery when they
lemming the asphalt.
Lemmings seem to me a myth.
The tiger is elsewhere.
The snapping turtle is a german submarine
with such armor and appetite.
The other turtles are painted;
and the women.
The badger is obviously a republican.
The wolf is above all.
The elk has a funny voice that
makes his penis bob, but the best
flesh for the barbecue.
The eagle knows everything
about carrion.
A frightened vulture will vomit on you.
It will eat your clothing.
Clothing is for winter.
The vole will not be caught
with peanut butter.
The mouse wants you to think him
a vole.
The shrew is the one who eats.
The tourist is the one that sucks.
The porcupine is too slow to mention.
The hyena is on the geographic channel.
The geese shit, and mimic a traffic jam.
The skunk smells like good dope.
You can see moose, but they will die.
Otters taught me how to play with
children at the beach.
The catamount surprised me when it
screamed like a women
that I tried to woo.
That's who!

I find poems at the bait shop
hiding like hopeless minnows
or fiction pertaining to
the big one

in the ionosphere of lofty notions
perchanced upon at the grocery
on Owsley's potion, even rubbing
lotion on a crone's feet

I find them among Jack's animals
parading through my stereo
on the the prerequisite Saturday trip
to the Wal-Mart poetry section

even basking in the late summer
like baby seals that don't
smell the blood on the
surface of everything

I find poems in rivers
that know the rhythm of a woman
just before she, she she, sings
to the moon, with a shiver

In sweatpants in american trailers
in a tailor-made nightmare
that reminds me about the meter
of the poor, the failure of capital

I found some in the biker bars
behind bars, beneath my scars
in the rising sap of Mars
and in those nocturnal lights

I found a rhyme in a hymen
but kept it to myself so as to bait
another mate with silent respect
that Aretha taught me

I even bought them in books
that poets and other miscreants
wake me with before the hungry
treadmill eats me daily

On the blank daze, I just
closed my eyes
and wrote about what I saw

then

I finally pared a poem to two letters

NO

the biggest little word

applied at high volume by the meek
to the muzzles of those who seek power
in the name of a blameless albatross

A lie can never be quiet
but the truth can never be
too loud

The mountains and the moon, you see
alight with weight on the center
of me to gesticulate with waving arms
and chant the wind's vast secret

These breasts, these documents of god
release me from the we, the progeny
of such hungry mathematics, such
gluttony in the very eyes of sky

to view this melody of circles
held aloft by the breath of poets
that lurk in the song of forest
or the refrain of the sea

and thus remit this dim magic
of words that paint such limbs
onto the lips of a family tree
that so neglects this garden

and urge them to flee those
cities, those dollars, that choke
our blue with skeins of gray
and weave a carpet of farms

to soften our steps
and lessen our harm

I found America lurking in an idea
for a tattoo
a scalloped border, square, with
a Bo in a boxcar

a boxcar on those tracks
you know, down by the river
betwixt the water and
the highway
with 13 cents in the corner
down low on a woman's back
a REAL tramp stamp

but preachers are paddling the cars
to nations that bleed oil
and my ink is getting darker
my box, too small
and nobody knows the women
are queens with the power
to heal those soft men
that only grow money
and demands

I defined irony on the wall
of a stall with promises of luck

"I beat up a redneck today!"
"I drive my Prius to the airport!"

but they won't get it

That train knows things about America
with it's calluses, sweat-brimmed
gimme-caps and Friday night

The train watched the neon build cities
without calluses, maize, or real
folks that eat the fields
and paint the very sky
with commutes and
propaganda

The cities grew lawyers and
futures traders, which trade
human lives for green papers
and lovely professional
wives

The long dog hollered with soldiers
and cringed with blued women
running, but we had a card game
in the back with brown bags rustling

The rivers still slouch to the delta
on that wee tattoo from
a land of bars with
gravel parking lots
and grain elevators
taller than the banks

The woman who wears this stamp
will describe, with her hips
the circle that ends back
in America

I sat with Boxcar Willie once
I bet he knows her

I got these circles
   from Pa that hurt
   an' hurt
   when i'm too small to love, an'
   it was like that
   in the 50s

"YOU WORTHLESS BITCH!"

to salve that weak muscle
   with all the power an'
   glory that sends our lowest
   common denominator
   to the tribes with

guns instead
   of our highest with ideas
   but when i'm high, she don't
   make me hurt her

back
   and i'm so hard to love
   so hard, and what she
   can't give bounces
   like sunshine from
   a white wall with

fists

I got this forgiveness, this
   shame from her, that
   showed me a stronger light
   which chatters with angel

voice

that is made up of breasts
   and permission

to find a staircase, to kneel
   in ripples, on a pond
   where tadpoles swim,
    unafraid

and sew the seeds of circles
   that may rise from
   this abyss, into the
   round and trusting eyes
   of a child with softer

circles

Callused Hands

When you shake my actual hand
you can tell I am real
These hands know the soil, the
mechanics of locomotion -

the world that leads to poems

These fingers are wrenches, the palm
a hammer

When they sing, with a flute
or tingling strings
they tell hard stories
with gravel in their voices

When these hands dance on soft
shapes, they are more profound
than a softer caress, more
certainly authors of a finished task -

able...

Her beauty hides like a shadow
as if a dove alights in the black
as her back is bent to weeding
all the need from her basket

in the blind eyes that fed
on Marilyn
in the bank that finds soft release
in the geometry of abstract silk
that is not real
but binds them so

she is not that grail to grasp, but
in the eyes of a poet she swims
like wheat or honesty
and the moon, her womb, her spirit
thrum as if the sun, a lost epiphany
arise in her silent song

Her loveliest gown changes color
with the seasons that leave
secret alabaster holidays
soft as the crows giggle
in the corners of the eyes
where I live

Martha is plain, like the soil
or the sky, wind music

She is ordinary

like breath

{For Darcy}

i name you empathy
that wears your black dress
deep in my very eyes
the nurse with the soft
cool hands
that hold me when I moan
verbose little hands
little fists
that hold her spirit tight
you write my never-son
to life
while I tape the door-frames
as if I hear him weep
and I look for you
where churches fail

we are refugees from
allen's lost battalion
that meet in stanza seventeen
to howl
you are in my mouth
when black pearls scratch
at my teeth
gathering themselves
like grandpa's german consonants

i would dwell in your bell-jar
to moot mute misery
when dark stanzas build
like lead on the horizon
i am not her
but my arms
my forest
hold you both close

dear girl
i hold you close
in a soft pouch
with a lock of hair
a poem for a never-child
a hug for her
a dried orchid
a pinch of earth
and hope

no black-cat-bone for me
i am visible
entrails gleaming like poe
for you
dear girl
i will be no Sylvia
no anne
but work that tired bellows
as if I could burn
with a fire like yours
that wakes my pump with lightning
that heals my scars
and paints my northern sky
with lights that dance
among a million stars

i was praying
without a god
until I plucked you
like a willing rose
from a lush constellation
of stars
to show me how a spirit shines
in the dark
when chaste and loving words

collide

like ours

141 grams, floating,
   like a dradle from mars.
Bulldozers and merchants
   set courses and chains
   to capture your brothers,

but you fly free,
   a populist sort of bird
   scorning fees and
   upwardly mobile poseurs
   to flit through illegal breath;
   a rainbow in flight,
   tasting the spirits of dead poets
   and sea-gulls
   in defiance of gravity;
   a high-velocity reminder
   of the one circle.

You like dogs,
   but only large ones,
   sporting bandanas and soft grins.

You sing with a silent voice
   I hear like hymns.

You whisper, to generations x, y, z –

"Silly children,
   Hacky-Sacks can't fly."

, the others
do not conform to cubicles
who are the unsprayed apples
scabbed, and oh-so-red
with the benediction
of the sun
we are luminous with
peace and napalm burns
godless, yet we pray
we stutter on delete
confronting colonial bullets
the next line of a cantankerous poem
a frightened and
unspoken speech
asked to define currency, we
paint landscapes
of the orb we were designed
to inhabit
while farmer Jones plants
subsidies
and the Fox flickers with subliminal
teeth
we love humans who may be women
or not suspicious of glee
in the lee of pragmatics
who have shackled orgasm
to the Novocain of mc-mansions
with chains of blank bank notes
in the silent symphony of greed
and false yardsticks
try to plumb the distance
to a womb
we are broken, you see
broken on the wheels that crush
all the actual circles
that form with drums
wherever naked folk must dance
that design geometry
in the very sky

that show us the way around
the merchant
to the moon, and her distant tribe
we are broken like a wholesome
hymen in the wake
of stepfather number three
by what he takes
by the angry secret beneath
a priest's robe
that blocks the sun
like a blanket of ravens
the others bleed like mothers
that inhabit an actual clock
or pounded by a warrior's cock
resigned to this
we bleed on the battlefields of the clergy
of the patriotic entrepreneur
on concrete ribbons
stalked by steel dinosaurs
resigned to this
but we, the others
sing, dance, drink, fuck, laugh,
think, eat, paint
vistas that never existed
hitchhike all the way to brilliant
stanzas of truth that
can't be bought
(or sold, it seems)
we don't fake orgasms, but
repeat them
in abstract mathematics
to define O
we hear the rhythm that
marching boots obscure
we follow that heartbeat
to the river
and we bathe in a church
without a mirror

we never wrote a poem in a courthouse

but we wrote a million in jail…

When gravity has fastened ugly claws
and business has eclipsed the very sun;
just look, until you glimpse the very maw
of all, warm, in a web that magic spun.

I see the eagle, riding on God's breath,
high above the mother of waters, higher
than the geography of life and death
to rest, bronze, atop an emerald spire.

When the years bear down upon your shoulders,
and the wars resound in your fractured ears;
just listen, until your ears grow bolder
and let the sound most wholesome pierce your fears.

I hear the loons, at the end of the lake,
laughing about the poor economy.
I hear mankind's future, as we forsake
the money to study agronomy.

When the smog paints current existence gray
and the blue ball reeks of ambition's thrill;
just taste as wafting waves of rainbows play
across some distant plain, atop some hill.

I smell fireflies and innocence, grace
in the very face of war, a child's breath.
I smell the electric hum of blue space
and the bouquet of a circular death.

Look until you see, listen 'till you hear
the garden, whisper in a babies ear...

I sing to make you hear my tricks

Alone, I am a sunset poem, a plea
to raise your hackles, to breathe

my secrets
on the back of your neck

If you listen close, you can run with me

I impregnate your mere dogs
with wild thoughts; natural inclinations –

the joker that inflames

With my family, I am a symphony –
audible breadcrumbs on a path
that leads you home –

love songs, on the breath of night

Yesterday, I found a poet
in the forest -

a trickster

Now, I have stories to sing

and indigestion…

lives where my deck eats
                    dirt, an' flowers, an'
pillbugs 'n' such
                    but he eschews notoriety
like Buddha with warts an'
                    runs beneath the porch, where
anthropomorphism ends and
                    aforementioned pillbugs
hide without dogma
He suns on scabs of pine, where
                    rainbows stalk the sky
where shade meets new fire
                    an' I rain like actual god
I think he calls me "Big pink rain dude"
                    like Jobba the Hut, or
some cataclysmic event
                    when I water the colors of
an evenin'
          in some unknown toad
tongue that the humminbirds
                    don't hear
Beneath the cedar 'n' the tie-dyes, the
                    laughter 'n' spilled beer,
the poems, an' bad jokes
                    his luke-warm-blooded body blinks
at the thermometer, can't
                    even tell he has hives an'
the bees 'r' gone
I can't fit under there to take a
                    "amphibian meditation" 'r'
"a moist approach to Zen" class when Josho's
                    dog barks an'
he withdraws from the thunder
                    of dancing feet 'n' Modest Mouse
is turned up
          so we can't hear the world end
There aint presidents 'r' generals under there,
                    no priests, no white
cotton temptation, universities, churches, 'r' sin
                    just pillbugs, spiders, an elder
an' a circle to be heard by poets
'n' toads

Don't look at the mirror on the mattress.
Never mind the fifty-cent earthquakes, the
{ribbed for my pleasure} impersonality.
Never mind tomorrow's tears, weeping
like lubrication for secret hinges.

These neon moments flicker like a sign -
heartache for $29.95, extra towels - $5.oo.

These blinds remain closed, dust on the hope
and the rules on the door avoid fidelity.
Rocky Raccoon opened the drawer I avoid
and he knew my hope, my release, like death.

He has spilled like cheap gin again, the
circles spin like glass-rings on the bureau
and I'm only two plastic glasses, a foil
wrapper, nothing, really.

Gauze

I see the world and you through gauze,

{the pain, you see}

and am not seen by daggers
or marred by such lovely frictions
as companion or love,
not woven into any fabric but
this soft and threadbare visage.
As long as I remain ether
am I neither victim or crime
and only naked in a poem

"I never sat in a boxcar with Neal or played Mexico City William Tell
but I lived in a 1968 Ford Country Sedan, in the arms of America."

Me, just now.

I watched the American dream being eaten by the Supreme Court
as if Florida forgot Ohio, and the innocents bleeding our last freedom.
I did mushrooms with kaleidoscopes inside, heard Dr. Leary's calliope
playing songs for enlightened existentialists in a grand circus.

I caught the last train to bohemia in the waning of America, tasted
the lubrication in a vast machine of freedom, saw the titties freed.
I saw the great minds of my generation turn filthy with money and oil.
I rode a horse with a white mane that fed on innocence and freedom.

I heard the bassline of Hey Joe as a background to sex and death
while the dynamo of merchants spent those boys like ugly coins in
the defoliated rainforests of innocence in the cause of French Colonists.
I saw Nixon predict Ray-Guns, and burning bushes, scorching hope.

I was not germane, in my tie-dyes and peace, not commercially viable
with bare feet and odd prestidigitations, inspired by red men's cacti.
There were many angels on many roads, and they all tasted like glory
or multi-orgasmic tops that spun to songs that reminded our loins to
sing.

Boxcar Willie taught me the rhythm, but I was one of Jerry's kids
on Ken's bright bus to everywhere, and nowhere at all, a dervish,
wilding in the landscape of paisley and day-glow microbuses with
daisies and laughter, the scents of Rastafarians and rodeo sex

and it was good.

Rust and gray hair settle in as the road to bohemia is littered with
corpses
but an old man in a small garden still dances,
naked, except for Jesus shoes…

Today, Mother Superior was angry. I was reminded of war. Perhaps the conflict between liquid and solid, water and terra firma was the metaphor that bid my muse thus. I thought of the "walleye storm," with the three of us racing for shelter behind the strong arm of Long Island, the feeling of power and impending doom, the fury, and the foreboding of that simple, quiet draft card. I remembered Ohio, and my purple war wounds, gathered, not on distant shores, not in aggressive colonization, but in the patriotic pursuit of peace.

I remembered the day of the April wind, when I put in at Washburn in that innocent and trusting canoe, took out, {downwind and thoroughly frightened} on Little Girl's Point; hitchhiked forty-five miles back for the hippie-mobile with it's canoe rack. That wind subsided, but the voices of the burning bushes wreak havoc yet. The sky should have looked askance at the bombers as it did my flailing Napoleon arms, tiny with their wooden paddle, scraping at the sacred skin of of Gitchegumi-turned-beast.

"Tell the children I love them," I shrieked into the November storm. The boat had sunk behind me in the slough. It blew and blew, biting with teeth of sleet at my resolve to make it, somehow back to the landing. It was the month of big ducks, and the price of a shell would feed us all for a winter day. I tried to swim in the channel my wee boat had carved in the ice, but young strong shoulders were blown against the brittle edges. This was my Dresden! But where was Trafalmador? How would this insignificant pilgrim find safety? Nature was not my peaceful home, but a battlefield, {"To rest is to die, to rest is to die" was the mantra that plied that icy slough.} The police officer that found me trying to unlock my auto with frozen digits and a key in tight-clenched teeth was as handsome as the cousin I lost in the Tet Offensive.

The storms brewing in the middle-east feed the beast. Like the mushroom clouds over those distant islands, no celestial hands guide them, but the gather-hands of greedy men. Again, the cost of pride for men who hide behind pulpits and castles is the blood of the sheep that fall like the cotton faces of each hungry wave.

The storms of men are those I fear, and nature's storms are dear, because mother's skies always clear in the lee of her anger, and legends run clean. The wars, though, chew at the land with false mouths, armed with innuendo and sheep-chow. Will this storm be the end, like some whispered secret from a Paris cemetery, or just another big blow?

Eyes that see hands craft the actual, feet
that walk all the way
describe one path and this grand party.
Zones of misfortune are deemed
as if the pain seeks an address
or some pairing of odd nouns.

A draught of magic is moot for
men with responsibly absent deity with
shirtsleeves, rolled to face
friction on the handle of the
the   )
and wield it like destiny
in a sculptor's hand.

A poet ponders the
and bends it into an
with the stroke
of a body,
  now.

Before I Sink

like the last island into
the last sea would I write myself
in rhyme, I think
like red and yellow flowers
or a first kiss

the poem of me would
shriek like a stormy lover
or a river, slowed
by that first taste of ice

I will lie beneath three stanzas
birth, magic, and love
because all else

is irrelevant…

Oh, soulless seed of man, unholy war
that seethes through history like a pox
and lends young men to unholy chores,
desist in fitting young to flag-draped box.
Oh, trumpet, false and ever greedy, raise
your voice no more in cause of death
but lift it higher to announce peaceful days
as if mankind can sing with loving breath.
Oh king, oh preacher, full of spite
rescind your call to arms that so ignites
your sheep to sail abroad and fight
and raise our eyes to higher heights,
where the family of man shares one table
and wiser men weave sunlit fables
of a time when no more young men died
in the cause of old men's selfish pride.

Purple Days

The purple dot hit the spot in seventy-two
    with drum circles and holy dervishes.

Hugs were free and freedom ruled the forest
    where organic children played barefoot
    from head to toe.

Electric sunsets wove spells of chanting loons
    as we danced around paisley bonfires
    with love and breasts that breathed.

It was not moot that we danced
    before the innocence died.

To weigh the impact of the largest
grudge
or otherwise measure the mad-hatter's
antipathy or gauge
the temperature of frost on a soul

To organize the debt of evil
on the face of the wronged man, or
meter evil held for evil done
to place the weight in any
unwilling cart

To carry such as a martyr to the right
of wrongs in any dark knapsack,
in the climbing of light
from birth to some unknown rung

is moot

To fly, one must know the wings
of forgiveness, empty that knapsack
of all but love

that does not envelop its family in numbers –

in value or valiant endeavor –

but in need

If I fell in the forest
would anyone read the silent sonnet?
If I plead in magic meter, will
someone plant daffodils
on the fields of war?

If I paint icons of hope
in the tabernacle of words,
the final library,
would you plant love
for my grandchildren,
dancing beneath the stronger sun
of commerce?

When I feed that aged pine
between epitaphs like "Good Boy!"
and "beloved rabbit," will the wind
remember that I loved?

If I find my rest between the lines
will someone sing me like sweet soil
or laughing children,

or will I fall
silent?

Peaceful manifestos, like a drumbeat,
are whispered on the winds of forever
from children of a remembered earth.

We chant and rant through honest bullhorns,
through warmer microphones that pry
at the eyes of commerce and layers
of obese politics

like rivers of words that feel gravity,
weigh the momentum of progress,
the vast imposition of false cities
on the skin of a universal mother.

As a fatted calf drains the last teat,
we whisper verses of curses
aimed at poisonous purses.

Merchants of war are illuminated
by volumes of reality that plead
for leaders to remember our children
need a home too.

We sing like the red remnants of hope
that dance in circles, real as the sun,
the earth, the moon, the circles
that must close on greed

before the poems end.

The Sioux holds rainbows safe
until May, once they have carved
silver reflections, climbing
the great divide to spawn.

I will be waiting in that sunlit crease
where clear waters cleave stone,
trout spell romance, and a river
becomes a church.

Holy Pronouns

She shines in the garden, as if the sun
has found its muse planting seeds in the ground.
She is my earth, around which I am spun ~
a moon for a gravity most profound.

She bloomed like bluebells on the verdant shore
of a river where clear waters run deep.
With eyes like April skies and smiles galore,
she did not bid me fall in love;

I LEAPED!

I wed her at the waterfall, tumbling
into the heart beneath that white bodice.
She's led me through this dance of years, stumbling
over bumps in the arms of a goddess.

Now, as the years adorn her like a crown,
she dances yet, like starlight in a gown.

that gather around fleshy agenda
   with axioms for a lengthy pulse?

a prison of words to enslave/ensnare
   the thigh to a writhing in approximation
   of Jack's actual nature?

Am I faint from the vapor of breezes
   atop Rand's cliff, some small death
   on the moist breath of a goddess?

Then number me as supplicant, lying in
   Wyeth's field, hungry for a rumor
   of your love, your warm impression,
   my grail.

I need no bank but the trove in your gaze.

If my grin names me fool, that sings you
   like a river, gliding through my own
   Ameriky, then whisper me in kisses
   that know a robust patriot,
   be my nation.

And together, we will forsake these names,
   these frames that build our love
   suburban ranch styles and innuendo,

   forsake the games of parry and thrust
   to trust the only eyes that see us whole,
   to lie in the sun

   and see ourselves in the clouds
   like two gathering storms

      with one secret.

She rises like my morning sun
to illuminate the daily grind.
Her hair reflects like gold that's spun
on looms where distant stars align.

The flowers in her gardens grow
between vegetables and laughter.
Dancing, she winks, as if she knows
just exactly what I'm after.

Woman, mother, emerging crone
gliding along my sum of years,
she dances on feet that have flown
down to drown the rhythm of tears.

Magnetic north, she lights my way
to magic fields where poems play.

Experience

My only grail is friction,
    the texture of soft abdomen,
    the flavor of dew.

My bible is the waves
    that lap at shores of Xanadu,
    as you arch to me.

My church is in the map
    to laughing children,
    my hymn, your sigh.

I am callused; torn by time,
    and shorn of self by love,
    I am only me in you.

I live where the skin brushes
    the soul.

Oh, fallopian construct of sun, moon, and
magic
that spilled in mathematics and machinery
across my mother's face,

Oh, bipedal curse that builds vigorous
apothecaries, swelling the banks with poison,
with seeds of drought,

Oh, scurrying ants with wings of steel, REPENT!

The garden will make rain and green gifts yet
for the few who scorn ambition and numbers
to seek her verdant womb

but tombs await those who genuflect
before the lucre-bucket, with their broad backs
turned to that which truly ignites
stained glass rumors and maize.

There are drums to lead us to the moon, honest clocks
growing dim in silenced hearts that remember not
that no men are gods,

that war is not holy
that cash is not holy
that large automobiles are not holy
that merchandise is not holy
that angry men behind pulpits are not holy
that mansions of excess and servitude are not holy
that missionaries with big sticks and mirror-gods are not holy
that crusades with gods that invent guns and false sun are not holy
that the people at the door with pamphlets are not holy
that hungry flags and carnivorous maps are not holy
that jet airplanes inflicting wealthy feet on distant shores,
men who tax the poor to feed the rich,
Exxon, Phillip Morris, Halliburton, and the pope

are not holy.

That the earth, the sun, the rain that cleans the asphalt dynamo,
the corn, the children's dancing, the sound of a beating heart
or water, marching from mountain to sea with gifts for all between,
the birth of a day, a child, a storm, a peaceful notion, the definition
of melting clocks by woman, moon, tide, that all encompassing
shape of all things, the circle,

are all holy.

Oh, man
Will we ever learn?

Zen and the twenty dollar bill

In seventy-three, I gave
a beggar a twenty

and the rush spun me
in circles.

Currency is an odd device
to employ

when fishing for

enlightenment.

It was a Dali-esque sort of morning. As unbidden clocks bid me wake to pursue green paper in the wilds of commerce, I sought solace in bright images. The forest embraced my steel horse with reaching arms. The breath of a living world rounded the window to infuse the spirit with blooms and wholesome rot. An odd sort of morning, the kind that does not stop for a newspaper, but swims in vistas, rays of light, bent just so by the nicotine varnish on a poet's windshield, a bright morning, dancing without coffee, wearing time like a costume. The gnomes had broken free from my dreams. No bank or café penetrated this magic window. I couldn't hear the chainsaws or the republicans.

As I crested Long Lake hill, the sun seemed to be eating Madeline Island. There were a bazillion million diamonds decorating the countenance of Gitchigumi, stirred by the breath of endless pines, whispering across brownstone teeth. Once again, the waters were plied with long canoes, singing voyageurs and happy red fishermen, free again as years shed like down from a nesting loon, singing just for me. No docks or stinkpots, no captains of industry in sailboats full of plastic francewater bottles and Birkenstocks, but bronzed arms, paddling birchbark boats to heaven. My eyes tasted a Wisconson, free of Missionaries or profit, smokestacks or metropolis. If this was madness, it was a welcome madness. Given the harmony of Loon and voyageur, I was glad the old Dodge sings bass.

The town failed to register with its art galleries and fancy breakfasts, sold to the cities that eat this last wild shore with a hunger for my dreams. There was a traffic jam at the lagoon beneath the Sioux River bridge, nesting geese, honking in the blue road to watercress and wild rice. I saw the steelheads, invisible beneath the escape of the Onion River, eluding the gravity of hardwood hills to tumble into the mother of waters, the sunlight, the chromium arch, the rose gleaming on their flanks; all clarified by moving water that mocked time and agenda. The fiddleheads parted the last vestige of autumn with tender green fingers. The wild asparagus was up in the orchards as I climbed the hill that brought the Apostles into view. The morels would announce the apple-blossom-time in two weeks. The laborer was on the way to work, but the poet was on the way to a sonnet, in very bright colors and dungarees.

{For Pat}

It requires no particular place to flow,
no respect from the land it feeds,
no song of itself for ungrateful ears.
It cannot be damned by merchant
or scoundrel, by grasping claws
of those who cannot inherit
the magic of the moon, the clarity,
the wisdom of water tumbling
over the smooth stone of time.

 The paintings I sing,
the vistas of poetry I paint,
the story that tells me, line the banks
like wildflowers that usurp a neglected park.
All seasons reside along this rhythmic
ribbon of thought, This Stream
of consciousness.

 If you listen, you can hear your spirit
sing like my loon, my coyote, my
laughter and tears.
There is a bend on this chromium path,
where sunrise kisses each mourning
with a hopeful mouth, hungry for you,
where a forever stone creates an eddy
that defines peace with silent song.

 Can you hear the ripples, from the stone
I have tossed for you?
This is the place light goes to play
with water and time is not.

 This morning, I built you a bench there.
It is not an ordinary bench.
It will take you to your own stream,
lift you from unwanted time, place, and company.
This bench can fly.

{for Allyce}

Your pomes cavort in my psyche
   like rays of light from a
   distant window
that turns rain into diamonds
   that wed me to phrases
   of innumerable nomenclatures,
all hard softness
and wet kisses from a cloud, a
   blunt instrument.

They invade me like a subliminal earthquake
   that stalks the staunchest foundation,
   probing for cracks,
finding the ones with the keys
   to my mother's spine
   like warm nurses with hammers
and therapeutic appliances.

Your metaphors make a bison of me,
   wooly, and nearly extinct,
   domesticated, and

burn down all my fences
   with the fire of deeper verses that
   alight in the dawn of my eyes.

Vessel

My skin is the sack
   that holds me, molds me
   to the shape of man,

that bends me to a sigh
   on soft lips, an earthquake
   in a womb,

that spreads a quiver
   like rings from a stone
   across a pale pond,

that bears the scars
   of missteps and lost love,
   that weeps.

I am stored in this vessel
   that sails on stormy seas,
   intent on a caress,

and my only grail
   is friction.

Experience

My only grail is friction,
   the texture of soft abdomen,
   the flavor of dew.

My bible is the waves
  that lap at shores of Xanadu,
    as you arch to me.

My church is in the map
  to laughing children,
    my hymn, your sigh.

I am callused; torn by time,
  and shorn of self by love,
    I am only me in you.

I live where the skin brushes
  the soul.

Death

I live where skin brushes the soul,
  in the meeting of foot to earth,
    the answer of man to tides.

I poured myself into woman
  that I could visit holy places,
    cavort in a fleshy circle.

As I savor the wiser dermis of crone,
  and dance to slower drums,
    I choose my bed,

beneath the tree that reminds me
  there is more to a tree than bark,
    and saplings need room to grow.

Retirement Fund

I save children's laughter
In my void against
Serpents
And thin sand

{for Walt, Allen, and Robert}

A homeless soul is but a wraith,
    an uncharged ion on an empty street.
Writhing in the grasp of fleshly faith,
    may spirits sing, and auras meet.
Profane! Profane, the pimps of war,
    who count the dead and living flesh
    like lucre in some vast department store,
    as waves of farmers sons are threshed.
I love them all, these sheaves of soul,
    the baker, at work in the early morn,
    the first woman, blackened, mining coal,
    the bicep of the farmer, hoeing corn.
My friend is an organic farmer,
    with five young children, little money,
    but he sings inside his callused armor,
    as his lips are smeared with clover honey.
I love them all, the chubby cherub, the
    mother's breast, the magic fountain,
    an ebony back, once bent to the lash, a
    chanting Buddhist, atop a mountain.
A man's body is a sacred thing,
    with thighs to lift, and hands to build.
A woman's voice was made to sing
    of secret temples the moon has filled.
I love the electricity of the brain,
    the womb, the breast, the turgid nipple,
    the hips that articulate the pain,
    the pleasure, quaking in rising ripples.
A sculpture holds the very soul of man
    in a poem of flesh, staunch but yielding
    to grand designs and simple plans
    the soul of man is prone to wielding.

I've been early for everything

A November baby, born
at the equinox

a lover of fruit that is tart

of lovers, granted access
to a vulnerable sort of

divinity

too soon, too soft

like the flowers the frost burns
before the sun centers
on mourning

They all blew in like early gales
with the scents of wombs
and wet leaves, of hope

but, riding the harbinger
of winter, they grew
cold to me

temporary

Sleet rattles in their passing
against the panes in the window
of my poems, the verses
of curses at the dying of the

light

the conquer of the day
by the coming night

And like November, garbed in fine
colors and rotund with blessed
harvest, I seethe with change

I angle for fat trout
in the sea of tranquility, unkempt
in my pursuit of amniotic fluid
before I am painted like a frieze
on the walls

of winter

Early, that season of waiting will
plant me near the garden
in that soil, that November

that smells of
wombs,
wet leaves,

and hope

Lets Go To The Hop

The bass, rhythmic gyrations

Sweat on perky flesh

Whisper, cajole, fondle

LUBRICATION FAILURE!

REJECTION!

Remit ego

Curl in ball

Repeat.

{For Gregory Corso}

I scrape the detritus of deceleration
and an otherwise rather mediocre assemblage
of organic chemistry from my bed
to observe another circle of the decline.

I am a poor man; all I have is the moment
to jingle in my pocket as if it has a denomination
or gravity,
                when it's always taking its leave.

What weight then, clocks that my doctor
shakes in my face with a scrip for Chantix
and x-rays of my last book, with
short rotund lines and time to "pink up"
at a reading?
"Simple as a fry-pan," I mumble, stuttering
across the actual floor with Charlie Chaplin steps.
It is not moot to ponder; really delve into the minutiae.

{Thanks, Jack, for the whole not moot thing.}

There is elixir, and poems, chanted on the porch with music.
I look out, out, until I discern visions.
I listen until I hear whalesong from Melville's grave.
I raise a drinker's nose to ingest the molecules
of one fleeting nano-solid in the repeated versicles,
{all ooohming, and shit},
kiss the sky with a proud probiscus to
taste the breath of the world.
In the waning of the momentary reign of a
blip on a screaming radar called wordslinger,
philosopher, asshole, or grandpa, one naturally looks ahead.

But I see bastions of scurrying/cannibalistic/ants,
praying to entirely too many rosy deities,
while they brandish antennae at one another
and build a monumental magnifying glass.
I hear thunder, and the fabrics of reality, of
my grandchildren's tents, are torn by careless hands,
and I smell burning.

A Different Sort of Blue

I am a different sort of blue
that prickles with gooseflesh
when the sky paints forever
deep into the lake of me

Sighs and scythes share this
when the light sings
like troubadours
struck by obtuse beams
and odd geometry

Anne drank too deeply of the hue
that crept from that exhaust
with false promises, whispered
azure innuendo with
clenched teeth

Violet underpinnings bind me
to the cerulean orb that
may otherwise

spin me off

before I mix the color of god

Space Travel by Out of Body Experience

Above the faint architecture of man,
like a dove or a saintly astronaut,
devoid of fleshly uniform or plan,
deployed on wings my merest notion sought,
I plied the skies of evermore, adrift
on potions that open my mind so wide
that stars zip past my embryo to sift
as grains of time the hourglass can't hide,
and though I didn't/wasn't matter, whole,
I yet applied myself to flit through space
like an albatross myth in a black hole
or a constellation, shaped like my face.
Behind my eyelids, is a greyhound bus
with plenty of seating for all of us.

somehow, despite the dogma of cogs
   my mind yet sparkles

i intended for my path to rattle with boxcars

boxcars that clickety-clack with
   weed, enlightened verse, cursing
   the landscape with Mexico City
   William Tell and rumors
   from Tangiers
but the woman had breasts and an ear
   for poetry, a noble soul, and children
   with mortgages; hungry mouths
   and minds,
   {oh, those gleaming minds}

the factory did not gobble the green thumb
   that hitched all the way to commerce
   with a mullet and tattoos beneath
   the republican disguise

last year, I made enough cash on my poetry
   for a damn good bottle of tequila
   and called it macaroni

The Mother Earth News lied about what
   my five acres would do, with chickens
   and lots of Bic pens
  but there are forests and vast rivers
   that sing in a poet's ear like
   an x-rated lullaby

i had a recurring dream, where poems
   were money and there was
   no currency for war
  politicians plowed fields, maidens danced
   and I woke up

   sticky

had a full name in church
that sounded like maam
or Finlander royalty

on the crick
when the steelhead were
running like young pups

on the ice
where she called me boy and
poked fun at my gas -powered
auger

while she cranked away
at - 30   thirty inches of ice
three holes

but

in a hand-tilled garden
that fed a village

I got to call her Mae

The hand that baited a hook
was ninety winters
strong

Those vegetables taught me truth
in no uncertain terms

Her pantry
its ball-jar rainbow
rendered banks humble
in my poems

Her songs brought Ireland
to a Tennessee that never
left my feet

I helped Mae lift her man
those last few years
and she helped me
find one

inside

Molting

{for my brother, the Sparrow}

Cities rose to absorb the sparrow
with dingy spires and poisoned seeds.
Disheveled, wet, cold to the marrow,
with a hunger no magic could feed.

Craven before the beaks of ravens
that tore at him with dogma's beaks,
he sought a nest, a circular haven,
a palace for the hungry, the meek.

There seemed no respite from the storm,
no warmth for sparrows with weary wings,
or food to raise his earthbound form,
no psalms for a tiny bird to sing.

In the time of the molt, he found his wings
to soar far above the reach of kings.

The pile by the pet cemetery is getting too high
    like the driver or the national debt
They were going around and around in Florida
    but the only pony in the race was the mare
    and the Viagra Chevrolet roared
Point six miles, up the left, down the right -
    never mind the middle baby,
    it ain't for thinkers or poets
All the sheep were in church as the bank
    in the birches grew like roundworms
    in a pup or judgment in the pews
    and the news was all bad on NPR
The drift on the right accumulated soil, as if
    the edge digs for the scent of hell
    or oil to foil the caribou in Alaska
The bald tires of poverty spun to grasp the slippery
    slope with a full load in the upside-down
    vee of iron
    butterfly on the oldies channel, loud
    and damn, that snow was heavy
    but two-hundred horses
    can push a lot
Careful 'round the mailbox, boy, the snail
    don't like the winter much, and the loggers
    fly by with loads of the national forest
    to grow condos in parasitic cities
    where they drink tap-water
    from plastic bottles, but
I choose my battles carefully, and yesterday
    I fought the snow
Because my truck ain't heavy enough
    to push war-mongers,
    merchants, or god
    and the human race
    was running in circles
    in Daytona

I heard them before I was even born
  like the beating of a distant clock
  or the voice of a mysterious storm
Before I could even walk, I heard them
  in the thunder that shook the plastic keys
  that dangled beneath a cracked ceiling
  in flat Illinois
When I was a boy, there was joy
  in an ace of spades, keeping my time
  on chrome spokes, even in the cymbals
  of moving waters over stone, until the current
  tugged open the burlap bag of puppies
  and master was a cussword when a drum
  throbbed in a broken chest, blessed
  with the rhythms of sorrow
The fourths of July painted the sky with wars,
  with the drumbeats of napalm in Viet Nam
The preachers and kings were playing with fire
  in a desire for larger maps and prophets
But there was thunder on Dr. King's mountain
  and the fountain of youth found the truth
  in circles of drums that pounded for peace,
  circles of hearts that beat in unison, for the sheep
  that the war-monger fleeced , like a beast
  at a banquet of battlefields

but I still heard drums everywhere

There were circles of drums in deadlots
  and lots of drums in the forest
There were drums in the winds of change
  that echoed from mountains in four directions
The beat rang round from moon to tide
  and sang from the muscle of heart
  and the hand of man to the skin of a beast
  stretched tight over the fabric of hope
I heard them in the ancient rainbow, splashed

across the rhymes of a circling earth
   by tribes that measure time in eons
In storms that beat brownstone cliffs with waves
   that seem to gnaw at god's foundations
In nations of men that remind me, again, and again
   that we only need food, shelter, love, and peace
That everyone has a ticket to the dance we attend
   and we can mend our family if only we keep
   the same beat that lives in a true chest
   and leave the greed behind,
   remind ourselves, we are all brothers

When my metronome finds the rhythm of heaven
   feed me quietly into the earth to witness
   the birth of flowers
No weeping, no funeral or melancholy feast
   no, just a bed, beneath the pine, and rest

Some dark night, when the moon is high
   and the sky has bloomed with stars
   lie yourself beneath it as the world hums
   with all its humble magic

You will hear drums

An Open Mind

There is a place in my mind
where I found nothing
in static synapses.

Having found this blank page,
I look outside
for a pen.

I am vibrant
as unexposed film
anticipating ink
the color of god.

I crested the hill to see a sacred fire
painting a path from the lake
to the island, and the very heavens
Nothing special, this morning
no breakfast in bed, no
chorus of angels or epiphany
no birth, rebirth, or death
just the sun, water, air

I arrived at work, to spy a sea of green
atop another hill, with a view of
Madeline, and the Porcupines
Nothing special this day
no hiring or firing, no big raise
no braless goddess, posing
just so in a shaft of light
just growing grass amidst the orchards
that spring from soil that smells
like oak leaves and history
and a call from my youngest
down in the city

When I got home, I went to the garden
to graze on maize and sweet-peas
peppers, and the sound of the creek
To have a dinner, an evening
to play with the puppy and visit
Nothing special, this evening
no expensive Tequila or lobster
no rodeo sex with an extra woman
involved, no humongous TV
or lottery win, no calamity
Just a garden, a creek, a family
a weather-tight home, a woman
who hardly ever throws rocks at me
and a sunset like a Dali painting

She came from Greece with a hungry mind and breasts
   atop a heart that beat for the streets of plain folks.

She took art at Saint Marts, where I picked her up
   with nicotine fingers and dirty dungarees.

Her pops was flush, so lush liquors burned in my throat
   that emotes the realms of bards in empty boxcars.

She came from that money to sup at poverty tables
   that sang to her with harmonicas and axel grease,

that served the watery stew between the cracks of hope,

that groaned beneath the need to cope with layoffs
   and candlelit nocturnes of unpaid powers.

I took her to the store where mommas troll for ramen
   noodles in an aisle that resounds with tasty nos.

I took her to the clubs where black men sing blue songs
   and straight-razors cut the last set short at half-past
   never on the factory streets of a town that bleeds.

She needed more, so I took her to the cockroach hotel,
   to gray sheets to stain with wealthy lubrication.

More, more, so I introduced her to boy and girl in alleys
   painted with the spray-can hieroglyphics of
   artists that never had a cell phone to call daddy
   to make a drop at western union and save
   them from Amerika, save her from her thirst
   for a reality that was only a toy, for a rich girl
   with perfect breasts.

I died once, for a minute
and I saw a light with no face, no name
but I missed it
when I turned back for my grandmother.

I lived once, for a minute,
in that light
when I delivered my daughter
from grace to earth.

I saw it in the forest, in the garden,
and in her eyes.
I even saw it once, in a smile
on a dying face.

I don't recall seeing it
in a city or a church, except once
at a funeral mass, when I spoke into a daughter's
tears, "You can do this," and her eyes
believed me.

I don't see it in the news, or
between the pews, lined with
judgment and guilt, or in the mosque.

I even HEARD it around a campfire
like a Bly poem, or a peaceful
manifesto.

I don't have a name for this light, no man's face,
so I gave it a handle to carry it by,
in dark nights of the soul.

I nicknamed it

grace.

I raise a flag that is tattered
to point it at merchants of doom.
Our king is mad as a hatter
and the flowers of war have bloomed.

I charge the castle with an upraised pen,
assault the fortress, again, and again,
carve new hieroglyphics and angry pomes,
specifically aimed to protect my home.

The poets rose back in the days
when we heard the dreams of a king.
Now the poets have feet of clay,
preachers of peace have ceased to sing,

"Aaall we are say-ying, is give peace a chance."

The stream of consciousness is fouled
by innocuous little lines,
gone are the voices that once howled
to ignite the collective mind.

Yawp with me, at the angry dogs of war,
link verbose arms to fill the shelves and stores
with that vast light that shines at human core,
to rain your message of reproach; "NO MORE!"

Be those loud voices that remain
committed to justice and peace,
write new psalms to raise that refrain,
HOWL that song like a healthy beast,

"Aaall we are say-ying, is give peace a chance."

{For Dylan Thomas and Jerry Garcia}

 I will not fade from this place
that grows weary of me
as time adorns my weary bones
with notions, no longer blind to grace.
I will festoon the winds of forever
with the leaves that fall
from the years of my open eyes.
The very skies of nevermore
will twinkle with stars I painted there
with a rainbow of impossible phrases.
This seed of mystery that energizes me
where mother earth caresses
timeless sea is no temporal beast
to desert in weary lines of death
but the fire that burns
in my bequest of rivers, rhymes,
and poems that stand taller
than six mere feet of form.
This is only autumn, and I,
but a dancer, to revive
wherever there be drums,
for I rebuke the urge to die
with wings I write myself

to fly.

My breath is a prankster
   that hurls its epithets
and adjectives at libraries
with the suicidal tendencies of
window birds at high
velocity
   that preens like a crack whore
at midnight at
the intersection of today and
nevermore
   that mines an albatross
from ancient wind
   that sings with bourbon vapor
and gimme-caps amidst
wine, cheese, berets
and tweed
   that climbs into obscure nooks
with pyrotechnic displays
and the metabolism of a dervish
on a quest for a lost
epiphany
or a warm arrangement
of female genitalia to whisper
profound secrets into
   that annoys clerics
and academics, editors
and other miscreants
   that only wants to taste
the flavor of truth.

Perhaps, poetry, after all

is only Listerine.

In this shell of dust, this antiquary
that wears my robust soul
with a limp and love songs,
I shed these dungarees of time
to dance across the sky with you.
I will shed my eyes to see you clearly
as a wisp from mergence of sea
and sky, where the moon grows
from your salty estuary
to moisten my eyes with dancing.

The fiddler crabs will scuttle across
hot sand like castanets to keep
time at bay while a distant poet
bathes in the song your heart,
sings with your own poems, your
toes, that curl for traction
on a spinning world.

And finally, this wisp that dances
naked, pale, lovely,
as if to grant the very sky fingers
to know the form that warms marble
with a sculpted dance of life,
to light the sky with secret songs

is joined

by a wraith, a swirl of unabashed
reformation, a shape-shifting poet
that breaches the sky with words
to paint you, dancing nude
in a constellation where
skin is a bible, and a naked
disciple waits.

When your river floods
with fish
or garden swells,
it is morning's eyes that see
the hungry.

No winged raven, preacher,
preening before reflections
in mirrors, in books
may raise that sun,
adorn the earth
with dew.

Renewal resides in a smile
on the face
of tomorrow's children
and when the rain
dimples the pond
with circles that
spread forever,

I hear them giggle.

If your glass is half full
share it with a thirsty
stranger and you
will be quenched,
sated and smiling
like you learned
a secret.

Sharing it is like rain
on your river
on a brand new
morning.

A Colder Winter

I've been singing
With too many wolves
Too many lamb stains –
Scarlet indictments
Rorschach the winter carpet –
The pages of my spirit

Too many fools dance
To the tricks of the fox
The bitch yips
The dog yaps
And the hen house empties
To dark agenda

There are frigid crystals
on the fingers of birch
and diamonds in the night
that do not adorn
my desperate howl

But in the arms of winter's
Whitest storm, I walk
And my tracks may yet
Reach the moon

Amniotic Tides

In the quickening
of tides and stormy sea
the salt of many moons
break in holy rhythms.

She arches on the shore
of evermore as
waves of future pass
to break upon her breast.

The west wind knows
her alabaster sheath
as she bears the ocean
a daughter.

BEHOLD this handsome corpse and know
   of miracles, of magic.
There were terrors turned sweet in the oldest blues-
   kisses that tore like wars at the painted and
   life-softened fabric, empty now of the electric.
My gifts for those not faint of heart, but wealthy
   with hunger for exultation etched on flesh
   that thought ahead to tell the tales in new silence-
   to shout of my consequential epiphanies, even
   through death's clenched jaw-

   who'd have thought?
A scythe, a sigh?
A wielder of both, a welder of twin steels of wonder
   and death.

What canvass better than a poet's shell, what museum
   better suited to the telling of silenced tales than this?

I leave them all for you, these mees, wees, these arts that
   muse carved so patiently on a tired container, these
   portraits and incantations-

   for that most odd reader that reads me well, that filament
   of wonder at my odd wee treasures.

A colorful corpse, indeed, will I bestow on the frightened
   taxidermist, {he says no to skinning a brother, still I hope}
   that thinks this heap the most ill of pranks, but burnishes
   a Green River knife to a sacred sharp.

These tattoos are the illustrations to carry my poem children to
   the lively eyes of tomorrow, to shock the orbs of sightless
   men with the electric all, the gorgeous simplicity of wonder
   in ponderous times.

Winter

When the Sioux is hung
with chandeliers above
invisible giggles
and snowshoes adorn
the clumsy visitor,
the sun pierces the valley
to pry at my eyes with
prisms.

Spring

It takes a steelhead
to catch a steelhead,
my wife says, as
leaky waders affix
frigid fishermen, who
seek chrome and crimson
rainbows, climbing the
rising sap on the granite
haunches of the
great divide.

Summer

Children and dogs frolic
in shallow clarity, framed
by fern and maple
in a crease where the
forest is cool, and
reverent picnics
leave no scars
and wet moss
shames velvet.

Salmon shed silver scales
on stone paths to
procreation and death,
to describe my own
autumn, softened by
layers of warm colors
that cushion paths to winter
and some of these leaves
set sail on singing waters
that carry them with eggs
all the way to Superior
and forever.

ALBATROSS III

Like Samuel's ascendant bird,
my burden sings with strident notes.
My guilt, expressed in simple word -
to rise to gentler air, to float.

As oil befouls our sacred seas
and new warmth melts the poles; Relent!
Relinquish merchant's dirty fees -
embrace our mother earth; Repent!

As concrete monsters belch black plumes
and hungry beasts on asphalt roam
the threat of our extinction looms -
but hope yet lives for round blue home.

It's not too late to love the land –
to touch this earth with softer hands.

In September of fifty-six, I made my way, slimy and screaming
        into the American landscape while Allen read "Howl,"
while French colonialists counted lucre and discounted French
        communists and yellow communists in the first Viet Nam,
while ducks asses fathered my generation, lubricated by Vitalis
        in the galvanized forests of drive-in movies in America,
while young Kennedys pondered speeches, and red buttons,
        and bomb shelters, and starlets that were a short way off,
while the small Illinois farm town could still be a collective
        of callused hands and warm hearts in the corn belt,
while daddy bought a good camera and guarded German beer
        while his friends groaned at frozen Chosin, killing commies,
while it was still all right to bruise a wife, a child, who failed
        to live up to a beer-soaked notion of Midwest subservience,
while my good mother labored that I may someday stalk
        microphones with unpopular truth and poetic expletives.

When I was a child, with scabby knees and celebrated jumping
        frogs in my pockets, and we were never good enough,
when we rode stingrays and shouted "CAR" for time out while
        playing football in the eight hundred block of West Virginia,
when Cub Scouts pulled taffy in the Methodist basements of
        churches, of churches, of churches that defined us,
of churches where we wore dogma in little ladders of lessons
        on little lapels with secret daydreams of white cotton,
of churches that drowned me in shallow waters where Jesus
        hid in pride and judgement, and judgement of me,
of churches that ignored the sunglasses and shame of battered
        wives and cowering children at fried-chicken feasts,
when they told me not to go south of Adams street in Peoria
        because it was colored down there and dangerous,
when I heard the whiplash of Alabama in the borders of street
        maps in Peoria and "Soul Train" made my feet itch,
when the battlefield of protest that integrated the eight-hundred
        block of West Virginia street was my basketball court,
when I first went on the road on an orange-crate, clear to
        the playground on University, where the "bad" kids were,

when I first kissed Cindy, first got high, first asked why of
      a church where men looked to mirrors instead of Jesus
when the first of my brothers died in French Viet Nam.

                    Part Two

When I was young, I found rainbows in other cultures, and
      Gods that existed far beyond Methodist judges.
I found questions that lived inside Lao Tzu's circles, but he
      had Machiavellian tendencies that made me wonder
      if it really was Josho's dog who spelled god Backward,
a sweat lodge in my Wisconsin, where wise ghosts danced
      in steamy contemplation and magic rhythms,
a land of black dancing, south of Adams, north of the cotton,
      where I owed an unknown debt to blue songs that
      wrapped me in guilt I didn't earn, but carried with the
      pride of eyes opened wide to the enslavement of kings,
      the rape of queens as cattle for Virginia,
a blues bar in Chicago, where I was the odd-color-out
      while Detroit burned and Aretha preached the word
      that gave me the key to a protracted love affair
      with music from distant deltas and a crossroads,
      with a single, sacred word,
a symphony of revolution, where bohemia was found in
      books, and tie-dyes, and poemsthatweresongs, and the
      release of dogma's vast weight, and vaginas and breasts
      that sprung free to announce the louder voices of
      women in a new frontier, and exuberantly painted
      non-conformity, and the words of Big Gay Allen, the
      smoke of Mexican weed, the acid that etched deeper
      folds in an itchy brain, the mescaline of Carlos, the
      heroin of dark Jim that left me finally, writhing, and
      weeping, and puking, and shaking on a four-poster
      in a mobile home asylum, with arms like oatmeal, and
      disco biskits and booger-sugar to ease the pain,
a revolution at the courthouse, where we fought guns with
      flowers like shattered warriors for peace in Ohio, to
      end the endless napalm and slaughter of poverty's
      sons, marinating in Monsanto's gifts of bent babies
      that would break the hearts of misspent patriots
      beneath the medals that celebrate sin as bombs that

burst in the air of July parks and we forget Mi Lai
    as The VA sends the broken heroes to live in
    cardboard homes with ghosts and twitching eyes,
a revolution of Mother Earth News Foxfire hippies who
    showed me the garden and the map to a farm in Tennesee,
a girl on a moped, Crazy Ellen, my first witch, who taught
    me about tides and drums, menses, and the moons
    effects on men with hardons for witches, around
    campfires in a new found forest,
a red road in that forest, with drums that know the rhythms
    of JackandBuddha's actual earth,
a revolution of thought, that freed me to believe that I am
    in church while trout fishing, in church, shaping a
    small and ancient tree amidst swirls of chaos gravel
    or grazing naked and shameless, innocent again,
    like a second chance virgin in an organic garden.
a girl, THE GIRL, over a pool table in actual Wisconsin
    with a free spirit, medicine for broken dreams, and
    defiance of the secret service guns at the first arrest,
a girl with a womb that would make me immortal, a muse
    to fill my pen, breasts to feed a daughter, and my
    future in her strong and gentle grasp,
a girl that released me from knowledge with the last contraction
    that eased a girlbaby into undeserving and callused hands,
a girl who stood tall in testosterone thunderstorms, demanding
    Aretha's magic word from a tie-dyed jester who needed to
    put down the Frisbee and go to work in the reality of
    an America where the merchant is king, the farmer, a
    serf and breeder of soldiers,
a girl with the strength of the Butterfly that decorated a
    redwood in the California of greed,
a girl that would stand up!

                    Part Three

When a poet turns fifty in the forest, with grandchildren
    playing in a September cornucopia on the equinox
    the peace of that circumstance should echo in poems.
But the songs of men, born on the warmer breath of
    Gods that man has forgot in the greed of commerce,

the wars and wars and wars of whores of Babylon reach
    for the sons of poverty still,

the scores of peaceful preachers that beseech retarded Texans
    to release our sons from the responsibility to fill
    Halburtionian coffers with hero's coffins to feed
    soft pink men who shoot friends in the face and treat
    enemies with electrodes to two testicles until they
    confess to anything they want are labeled unpatriotic
    in act one of the death of the constitution,

the invisibility of Sudanese children, hungry and broken
    by rapists because there is no lucre for pale soldiers,

the image of Sam's Albatross as Jonathon Livingstone
    skyrat, supping on McFrys in a parking lot of an
    asphalt dynamo with piss-yellow arches,

the condominiums of Hummer driving, Francewater swilling,
    captains of industry that eat the forest to perch on
    the bruised brownstone shoulders of Gitchegumi,

the weeping of Martin's ghost at the sight of Dubya, hopping
    off the helicopter on day four to hug some brown
    folks for Fox newsbytes,

the pyramids of detainees, naked and posed for pictures
    to celebrate the victory of terror as diseased circles
    paint six million excuses for dead children in Palestine,

the saber-rattling sycophants with fingers caressing buttons
    of a hundred, hundred Hiroshimas while they masturbate
    in white houses and desert castles,

the only American voice to shout warm warnings emanates
    from a block long limo in front of a ginormous mansion,

the cities reach diseased claws ever closer to my son's farm,
    my grandchildren's future, grasping at the last clean places,

the melting poles make it hard to leave my grandchildren
    the hopeful poems they deserve.

Part Four

Half a century of unanswered questions add up to a vacuum that
    even now may grow the seeds of hope.

The steeds of greedy commerce may yet shrink as the ice
    melts faster in the bourbon 'n branch of good ol' boys.

The green of corn, of spinach, may become a new old currency
    as scraps of mathematics become paper for poems

and the soft hands of merchants learn to grasp a hoe.
First nations may revive themselves, despite the guns and Gods
    of missionaries, to teach the tribes to unite in the defiance of
    Babylon, and touch the earth with gentler feet.
My grandchildren know the dancing laughter of creeks and
    mandolins, the wealth to be found in a sunset.
My son knows that wealth is measured in the laughter of
    his children, and not in the size of his entrancer screen.
My daughters are strong in the truth I have not denied them,
    that they must be patient in their teaching of tides
    to men that know only the thunder, to teach them
    the value of the rain, to expect, like Aretha, respect.
My wife knows the spot, between the gardens, beneath the grandfather
    Pine, among the weathered boards with "Good Boy"
    and "Beloved Rabbit", etched in our families history,
    the spot where I would feed the land that fed me, beneath a
    weathered board that only says "peace."
        { a board I'm carving now}

Until then, I'll be the loud poet, the angry poet, the stalker of midnight
    microphones, with a bludgeon of truth so ugly it just may
    awaken the sleeping consciousness of a shrink-wrapped society,
a wordslinger in the cause of the earth that feeds us all,
a pompous metaphysician in an enormous clinic of words, imperfect,
    but unafraid in the denunciation of the dragon of war and
    the money-fueled race to our own extinction.
I will rest, finally, as a peace corpse beneath a pine tree, near a garden,
    having left volumes of breadcrumbs behind.

An Open Mind

There is a place in my mind
where I found nothing
in static synapses.
Having found this blank page,
I look outside
for a pen.
I am vibrant
as unexposed film
anticipating ink
the color of god.

The Mother Earth News showed
my father this place
where razzle-dazzle-berries
dance with dandelion and
good folk in sweet wine

This good earth where generations
twine like vine of generous zucchini
Where potatoes wait for venison broth
and sweet corn knows our smiles

This land that gave young men
to seven wars knows peace
and the poet with the hoe knows
green papers nourish not

Cycles of man ebb in actual nature
As man feeds soil, feeds man, and
heavy horses know patience
is strength

In this land where rain makes dancing
And the moon, herself has many names
Crops grow tall, and children, the
garden feeds the soul of man

Soul of earth, soul of man know psalms
of sustainable serenity in this place
where future and past are merely
cycles of germination

was purple, and green with envy, but he
    knew many ebullient limericks.
Others had grown wings of rainbow gauze
    to seek higher principles
    but he had found his eden
    where odd leaves, chewed
    could fashion bright chaos.

His garden was populated by roses, stone,
    and eastern mystery, fables
    and unicorns.

There were paisley giants, whirling to
    drumbeat and flute, to psalms
    on giggling breeze.

A white dog with a red bandana licked him
    and ripples of glee announced
    the length of contentment.

After all, dogs don't eat caterpillars, and

    hippies have the best gardens.

Black Morning

The abyss looks back
with the eyes of a frightened child.
Obsidian stones rattle
in breath that sucks
at the night with crusted eyes
that yearn for light.

Kings brighten the blackest day
with bombs
and morning will not find me...

They were all bright.
They loved to dance, my opium, my
pretties, and they made me
exuberant, like a
paycheck with an extra digit
or a pretty, spunky face.

With tiny, cool hands, they
molded my clay into
intelligent nomenclature
and grasping hips
as I poured unwritten
poetry betwixt
thornier stems than
simple rose.

I asked the seventh angel
"Why Me?"
But the answer made me small
and the residue of love
is fisticuffs, tomfoolery,
and any pain more simple
than tears.

All my angels swallowed
my seeds of discontent, my
loudest deeds, that
aching need to seek
that forest, that nexus
of yin and yang, of
heaven and hell.

They tasted tasted like sunshine
and do.

"All night I rose and fell as if in water
grappling with a luminous gloom. By morning
I had vanished at least a dozen times
into something better."

> Mary Oliver, from
> "Sleeping In The Forest"

A Winters Night In Bayfield County

The thin fingers of oak scratch on frosted
pane in the crystal clang of silent night.
Like the wretched claw of remembered pain
my little girl writhes.

It is in the cold of forest dark that he comes
to me, blanketed in the white of lost
hope. Bones chill with the unbidden ghost.

The midnight crash of bursting tree anoints
the forest with another monolith to winter.
Even the coyote who sparkles song to
frigid air proclaims this dirge.

But the sheltered seeds await a feathered
morning and song of chickadee, of
light, and the forgiveness, come to late
to wrap him in it's quilt.

And the song too, of narrowed brook
caresses watercress that defies blue tooth
to wave in liquid embrace, to grasp
smooth stone.

The pines, with heavy burden, stand as
sentinels against another monochrome eve.
The scent of pies, the length of me, supine,
await the moon's knowledge of me

and I forgive the winter...

They etched my mind with oils, images
  that take years to dry, textures
  of sable and moonbeam.

My lovely ghosts accumulate, like leaves,
  shorn of oak to fly away, and
  yet remain.

With a secret moan, a glance, or dancing,
  barefoot in far off evenings, scented
  by lavender and mystery –

they live forever in tears and sad grins,
  in metaphor and tangled sheets,
  in night sweats.

I found them in museums, gardens; I
  read two in holy pages of wounded
  butterflies and no relent.

My heavens opened and stars remember
  the first to possess my quill, to whet
  an appitite –

for love poems and lovely ghosts.

To battle guns with truthful words
and sheath rattling sabers in
greedy hands is my small voice heard
shouting in a garden of sin.

To shine good light on darkest deed
my poems pierce the breast of kings.
I plant my garden with bright seeds
of hope to which my children cling.

I will not fear those shallow men
who would reap a harvest of blood
but fill my simple forest glen
with a river of words in flood.

My cavalry has ears to feed
and language is my earnest steed.

Another Homeless Christmas

No mistletoe beneath the overpass
where only the thunderbird sings
No glory for the heroes of the past
No glimpses of a newborn king
No tinsel in a home marked "fridgidare"
or gifts for the children of strife
No popcorn in a park where no one cares
about another FUBAR life
Johnny got a gun, wrecked his freakin life
He only wants a stocking, hung with care
The Mad Dog has become his only wife
since he left his other foot over there
No Volta, No Santa, for homeless men
We forsake them once, and now again

The forest rages early now
apples, fallen like red golf balls
remind me to grease the snowplow
frightened by a new sort of fall

The man-made drought changed everything
green leaves fall like ill-spent money
no more bees and no more honey

but rainbows fall and children sing
within quilts of orange and red
Skeletons of death connect themes
bouquets of green from trees who've bled
new growth to sponsor darker dreams

As mother dies to craft this quilt
my mirror holds the key to guilt

Pumpkins, trucked from lands where it rains
grow smiles to leer at tiny sprites
and pan plays flute in odd refrain
to ease the earth to her good night

I would to wake Sam's albatross
to cover mother with gardens
to regain the fields we have lost
to earn celestial pardon

As winter's sleep creeps near to earth
with winds that blow so strangely warm
and wars consume her great blue girth
I fear the shapes winter will form

We men who pray to asphalt gods
have spread on earth, a quilt, quite odd

Those warlords of fire and brimstone preach
of high crusades, ideals, and lofty goals.
But mining farms for lads to fill the breech
of armies to fill their coffers and holes,
they hide behind banners on distant hills
as paupers die to fill their banks with bills.
With elegant speeches for boys they crave,
they lure the innocent to glory's grave.
Odious tyrants with flags and "ideals"
comb lower classes for patriots, fuel
for vast graveyards as worms await a meal.
Why is power granted to those most cruel?
They invent new Gods to justify hate.
Broken young bodies are boarded in crates.
They burned the midwives to glorify God
and buried their bodies 'neath England's sod.
They killed the red men who knew the mystery.
They harnessed the sun to fry whole cities.
'Tis the same men who falsify history
to glorify their cause and feign pity
for the widows and orphans of men spent
in endless wars with no peaceful relent,
in endless wars to expand their riches
by dying alone in bloody ditches.
Now the bloody price, spent on distant sands
as modern soldiers break in screaming toil
and fight to raise the flag in eastern lands
are counted by the current price of oil.
The warlord stays behind in abject fear
as their minions very futures are seared
for the profits that prophets hold so dear
because God whispers in a Texan's ear.
When will wiser shepherds follow the sheep?
When will wise lemmings refuse to leap?
When will the warrior lay down the lance?
All I am asking is give peace a chance.

Though distant, I heard the thump
Of you, impacting the dumpster of the
As-yet unknown demise of my innocence
Freedom was such an odd name for you
Daughter and breast took on darker taste

Though I didn't know, and couldn't dream
The scenes, the time was nigh to resurrect
A life gone empty of dancing and shame
To paint on empty parchment, vistas of you
To re-acquaint my eyes to the smile you missed

I wrote you ebullient, with dancing and chaos
With moonbeams and even your weeping
Was, somehow beautiful, astride my pen
Your loss of innocence, bright in that field
Where an innocent lass lay naked to sun

And the grasshopper bit that gracious thigh
To plant the seeds of shame in holy girl
Could not eat away the grace of you, dancing
In gentler scribbling of verses to sing your life
Oh, wet comma, to paint you bliss, I sing

The love you lost, to paint you deeper shades
Of blue notes and the nuance of wisdom won
In cotton fields and false men's ministrations
To the maiden's form you animate in verse
I sing the time he found you there, the one

I draw wedding scenes, where father hands
Heaven to a simple country man with shoulders
To carry you to the Xanadu I craft of offered word
And gardens, in cleaner sun, devoid of gray city
Where magic blooms and you hold a daughter...

She has perfect breasts
and we writhe, happy eels
beneath the suns
of distant worlds
while innocents die
on public radio
I buy tokens at peace marches
so I can taste her warm church
as provocateurs of frenzy
dine on orphans
I listen to news at oblique
angles so music survives
and I shine on genocide
with lightning words
to drown out the screams
while my next stanza
sculpts nipples
to sharpen the breath
of an angel

The Tiara at the End of the World

I brought her a tiara at midnight
 to frame her face in absent stars
as scars of commerce obscure the sky.
I set her feet to rhythmic circles
with drums that thunder like tides
and voices that sing like rivers.
I filled a cedar chest with seeds,
poems, and hope that she will
show them the way home.
She is princess of the future
that germinates beneath the ashes
of ignoble kings and wealthy gods.
I brought her a seedling in my autumn
to fill her children with orchards
that begin at a grave, where
an untrimmed, unruly apple tree
will whisper poems
to cleaner winds
and bare feet will dance.

While the fox gobbles our eyes
with wars, commerce, and Paris Hilton
and the rivers run away from cities,
I write gardens, where she smiles.

The sky falls into smokestacks that
reach to god like claws that seek
my children with a smirk from
Texas or hungry eyes
that chew on Darfur and the Congo
and enjoy the Alabama nooses
with fond memory.

Still, I write rainbows and daffodils
that bloom despite the drought
that General Motors keeps in banks.

There is an America in my pen
where the constitution is not extinct
beneath the tread of a short-bus-riding
patriot with some dark Jesus
in a hairy ear, and the Loon still sings
the moon aloft from troubled waters.

The merchants have found my garden,
my lake, my forest, and compacted the soil
with Birkenstocks, Hummers, and even
eaten my verses with culture from
Minneapolis, in crowds of berets
that nod and drain wine from
plastic cups while they make
me lie with currency and shame.

Naïve water-bottles from France
bob in the wake of captains
of industry that set gaudy sail
on the face of Gitchegumi
to escape the cemetaries
they built for their children
in the great beast that ate the
upper Misissippi watershed.

I met her in the forest
and I was
rooted.

She connected earth to sky
like a rainbow or a
metaphor for butterflies.

Her voice was northwind, all
she-wolf and flowers, all
blueberries, decorating
smiling children.

Her feet caressed the fiddlehead
ferns in a spring I would
drink forever.

She was the maestro of
sighing moonbeams, of
my turgid rise
and she found my poet
waiting for her
in her womb.

Her arms, in dancing with the moon,
pointed to angels, dancing
for my eyes.

I knew my seed would find a garden
where an aspen shades seedlings
and words may dance with
an angel.

She is mature now
with hands that kiss the sky
and roots that bind the earth
to sponsor my songs
and my thunder.

Muse – ridden, bound to ride a metric pen
my spirit, soaring high on wings of mead
wrote to the Albatross, and back again
luminescent lines for painters to read

Stem to stern, this heavy craft carries words
to wrap round phrase into infinite verse
to slander prophets with truths seldom heard
to sing, to dance, to rant, to rave and curse

And thus, to heal, these mighty words would strive
to seal the rifts that rend the hearts of men
that boil in great cities, bound to dark hives
and paint those hearts a gentle forest glen

This softer quill, this voice, found in the wood
would scribe myths and Gods if only it could

Estuary

There are orphans in my eyes
  that gaze aloft
     for fathers

but only mothers suckle infants
  and angels plant maize
     and rivers

and her eyes,
  my lover's gentle stars,
  sing the melody of
    clear waters, gliding

over smooth stones that
  define the path to grace.

When your river floods
with fish
or garden swells,

it is morning's eyes that see
the hungry.

No winged raven, preacher,
preening before reflections
in mirrors, in books
may raise that sun,
adorn the earth
with dew.

Renewal resides in a smile
on the face
of tomorrow's children
and when the rain
dimples the pond
with circles that
spread forever,
I hear them giggle.

If your glass is half full
share it with a thirsty
stranger and you
will be quenched,
sated and smiling
like you learned
a secret.

Sharing it is like rain
on your river
on a brand new
morning.

Thanks, Monsanto
for the orange that defoliated
my return.

For the bent baby that sent me
to the V.A and the dead pills
after she paid for uncle
Sam's pride.

Thanks voter-man, for closing
the hospital and making me feel
this asphalt, beneath the wheels
of justice.

Thank you kind one, for the
change in a tin cup. The chance
to forget black pajamas, her
smile, and the lives of real men.

A wealthy waste needed a larger
Frigidaire so I got a new home,
movin' on up. The plastic siding
keeps us dry.

My Mercedes comes in a brown
paper bag, in a tired spike.
My penthouse is the numb.
I am magic, invisible to you.

But, you hate me, you purveyor
of product, you proud patriot.
"Get a damn, job!", you snarl,
but I make you feel large.

I am the sidewalk oracle, the
story you don't want; I'm the
conscience left out of you.
I am your shame.

This back room, this
sanctum of chaos, echoes
with the incense of 1968, the reek
of closeted bohemia.

There are tattoo parlor business cards
and obscure posters of antique
origins stapled to it's smoky skin.

There are goblins, dragons, faeries, and
countless tattooed skulls on floors and
floors of shelves.

Bourbon, Tequila, Marbs, and rumors
of absinthe decorate wooden horizontal
in silver flask, ornate decanter, ornate
poets, bound to dusty nouns.

Volumes of Frost, Poe, Kerouac, supply
gravity for verbose beards to comb for
hidden icons as poems, stacked on
poems nestle in illegal stacks
and smoke-ring verbiage.

Walt, on the wall with Einstein, looks
on with a twinkle in his labyrinth
eyes as electric friends fashion American
words and mourn fresher corpses.

Sylvia and Anne, from thunder roses
and buried nooks, confess the sins
that we adore, open the doors
to penitent breaths.

The burnt-orange shag bears paths
of two-AM enlightenment and
pacing's search for aloof rhymes.

Harley parts and Buddha share the
space surrounding a self portrait of
a demented wordslinger in
a silly millennium, looking
for a clue in the rubble
of a thousand philosophical
discussions between poets, loggers,
criminals, lovers and
assorted memorabilia.

In a dirty little room where helium
voices mend verses and spin yarn
of whole cloth.

The one room in Bayfield county
where madmen and concubines roam
loosed of numb restraint to laugh too
hard at incorrect jokes, to read poems with
anarchy and female genetalia, to

gesticulate like broken-winged Albatross, to
dance like those with actual feet, to
condemn merchants without green reprisals,

to eat good red meat with no effeminate
apologies to grocery store hunters, to

shout, to weep, to leap, to

live.

Tribute

Ghandi was a gleeful warrior, soothing
the dogs of war
with biscuts
of hope
shining like
truth.

when the levee breaks or Patsy
sponsors testicular menses after midnight
on a battered juke to loud epithets
from the back room with
illegal breath

Cries rise on bourbon tides in moments
like Normy or Sally Fields and black
leather smells like good sex

Strong men fold because one crazed dervish
trumps muscular kings from Mellon
to Cornucopia, from Red Cliff to Port Wing
A red Harley lubricates the gutter
Whisky lubricates a wordslinger
a wordslinger lubricates

bearded mysteries in blue denim and
Saturday night floss

black eyes, black lies, and three-am
divorces break like oily waves on
the southern shore

promises are gap-toothed legends
from Appalachia or dirty jokes
about nun and none

the south has nothing on us
but leather has vomit

and a six-inch avon lady roasts the
sandy coast

hungry for neon

they say we are all made of stars
and so is the dust in the attic,
with the bats
that are too

there is a window where those diamonds
dance among notions and old poems
the middle years pry me into that cobwebbed
receptacle of dead dreams and old love
to carve verses on an old typer
that gives my simple words the impact
of a dove against the frosty window
of time

there are echoes of lubricating maidens
amid the moans of the dying
and the drapes in the corner cover
my shame with art-deco hubcaps
and ribald jokes

when an ambitious constellation
pierces the gloom with a blue shaft
the air is translucent with ghosts
in hats that used to wear my skin

there is a large box where daddy
keeps the war and his rage
in the back, where Barbie shares nude secrets
with GI JOE and Ken is jealous

{but of whom?}
there is an old knapsack that remembers me
better than I do

it took me down many roads on long dogs
that ran all the way to 1979
and I bet it has poems in there too

all of my old treasures dry in this place
where they will see me
when it's my turn to shine

{for Rowan}

Her verses caress me, like soft
   fingers of a beautiful ghost
   beneath a waterfall that
   plunges into me and
   forgives my adjectives.

Her pen is a quill from a hummingbird wing
   writing in the blood of moons that set
   in deeper oceans that reflect the sublime.

Her sorrow leaks like petals from a valentine rose
   until the darkest knight has seen one diamond
   glitter as gold in the soul's wealthy pocket.

When her pen flies lightly
   my eyes do dance upon the page
   to spy her warmest entrails
   gleaming in a still life of words
   beside a vase of daffodils.

{for Nicole}

You are the bitch that finds
poetry arising from beards
or a quickie in a vestibule
like some dervish that derives
diamonds from discarded
mini-pads.

Every time I think I'm the
king of the daytime tavern
poem, the prince of phrases to
hang garlands in the Seven-11

I read you, and feel like a boil
on Buck's big butt.

When my pen paints the sound
of a rod-knock in an old truck
or the bouquet of last night's
love this morning, I know
you would have painted it
with richer colors.

You are the real Eskimo
with sixty-two words for slush
and thirty-one flavors of menses
or implied sorrow, without
spending a single adjective.

You spill grace like bodily fluids
that splash your readers with
the effluent of genius that stains
me like the week-worn sweatpants
on the fat chick in the check out

line at some metaphysical,
metaphorical Wal-Mart.
Knowing how you hate
poems about poetry, about
poets, in rhyme, with allusions
to better poets, this one's for you...

II

To keep me honest with better verses
and paint my eyes to higher task, you write.
Your poetry rings with must and curses,
from days of truth, and groping in the night.

The things you seek with a vulnerable pen
alight in my eyes, again, and again,
as if we all require what you lost
and drink of today, to defray the cost.

No exhausted Anne, or Sylvia's oven,
but a witchy chick, with a verbose coven
of words that lick my muse with fiery tongues
to sponsor true manuscripts from tired lungs.

Whenever my head gets too big for my hat
I read your poetry

and stop rhyming for awhile.

{ A De-Evolutionary Primer}

I saw a blood moon rise tonight
as if to devour the earth.
My mind did open wide in fright,
full of this harbinger's vast girth.
I saw the industrial age
eating wise cultures of yore,
with mirror-gods that feed on rage,
as preachers preach for more, more, more.
Place food in my collection plate
because currency fills no one.
I've come to know, however late,
the only god I need is sun.
The tribes that lost the land to kings
remember psalms our mother sings.

From their round drums and dancing feet,
that grasp the ground so well, I know
the soil, itself, below the streets
that metastasize where nothing grows.
Aboriginal cultures dance
in circles bankers never see
and for our progress to advance
the wise seek paths to backwards, flee.
De-Evolve to save mother earth
before the cities eat the farms.
Save the ancient mariner's berth;
join me in raising this alarm.
Capitalism is a disease
Help me raise the albatross; PLEASE?

When she left, Albert's guitar
    sounded dark and holy
    like a hidden bruise.

When she returned, Stevie riffed
    like faster pussycats or
    linoleum dogs, running
    quickly to nowhere.

Her shame is my Mississippi
    and mine is sung on the bent
    strings of a forgiving dobro.

I am only a sanctuary for the queen
    of the roadhouse, my song
    the sound of a hell-bound
    train, brakeless and blue.

blue notes on the breath
        of a lost city

The denizens of my mind
        dance like ethereal
wisps or angels
        on the breath
of a metropolitan midnight
Like creaking doors
  misspent orgasms
or the call of spent
    syringes
        they call in strange
tongues and sibilant
    whispers in moist
gutters.
In the orbits of mercury
    and terraplane
a harp plays a southbound
        freight
a thunderbird shrieks
    chords of
she left me's

and the factory spreads my
   ashes from concrete
tubes
Absent of neon
  and twelve-bar hope
my own nocturnal
   omissions flit
about in a concrete forest
  where the air
is thick with ghosts

Blue Pantoum

And the bluesman knows the ache
Of the misbegotten minstrel, sour notes
The tarnished angel, the toll she takes
Of muddy rivers and iron boats

Of the misbegotten minstrel, sour notes
Of bad women, bad men, and good dogs
Of muddy rivers and iron boats
The taste of blood, the color of fog

Of bad women, bad men, and good dogs
A fender sings in painful bending tones
The taste of blood, the color of fog
A cold heart in a heavy song moans

A fender sings in painful bending tones
As tapping feet keep punishing time
A cold heart in a heavy song moans
Even weeping may sound sublime

As tapping feet keep punishing time
The tarnished angel, the toll she takes
Even weeping may sound sublime
And the bluesman knows the ache

Behind the church with broken steeples
　　beneath a tarnished cross
　　rests the women who
　　obeyed

When eyes arose to stormy skies, to seek
　　Gods in mirrors of false men
　　the wings were pried from
　　angels

Behind the church with broken steeples
　　judgment issues from guns
　　in sharp retort to simpler psalms
　　of innocent men

When pulpits ring with calls to war, the whore
　　of Babylon beseeches the good
　　in simple man to darkest deed
　　to foul the name of Jesus

Behind the church with broken steeples
　　robes reek of greed and decay

A gentle prince of peace is dishonored
　　by men who would be fathers
　　of frightened children
　　as forgiveness
　　is lost to crusades
　　and crusades
　　and crusades…

A leather collar, cracked and worn
    round the neck of time;
    a green brass bell, silently
    sings of Octobers and silk.

Hanging on the garden gate to spell
    dog backward, to peal the sound
    of trust , and a freckled ghost
    dances yet through thickened
    throat of autumns, dim
    in yellowed pages.

Two weathered boards, nailed askew
    consecrate the soil where Drummer
    turns to vibrating marble, to
    essence of warm Grouse.

Two weathered boards, nailed askew

        ~ whisper ~

        "Good Boy!"

I just read "Howl" for the seventy-eleventh time
   and now I have to howl too.

Howl about the homeless, in boxes beneath
   the infrastructure of American commerce,
Howl about the veterans, the denizens of nervous
   hospitals, spit on the streets by budget blades.
Howl about the slaves, freed from tall cotton
   to kneel at the same throne that shot Malcolm,
   the same throne where shoeshine boys
   kneel under the feet of potentates.

I need to paint impressionist dragons, spitting
   fire on distant horizons to line the banks
   with ranks of misspent blood and flood
   the ghettos and fields with mother's tears,
To paint the great gray libraries with verbose
   declarations of militant mayhem,
Paint scenery for Abby's guerilla theater with
   literal interpretations of soldiers, tie- dying
   battlefields like bloody tokens for a fictitious
   freedom machine.

I need to recognize Allen's Moloch
   licking at the innocent flesh of children
   with the fire on forked tongue speeches,
To recognize the face behind the mask,
   behind the curtain in a red-white-and blue
   Oz, and reveal him to the sheep, show
   them the shepherd's teeth.

My pen will pound a mighty fist on paper
   pulpits and sound a resounding alarm
   to those proud patriots that gather around
   leaders that feed on the poor with promises
   to list them on a hero wall.

My fingers will tap code into the worldwide web
   to etch holy words of womb, of four winds
   that seek relief from the burning dinosaurs
   and seas that reek of poisons, find hope

in holy circles on a blue stone.   **145**

My poems will sing forbidden truth like worms
  that ferret out the feast in rancid flesh.
Truth about the death of the middle class,
Truth about men that harm men to glorify
  Gods found in crooked mirrors,
Truth about the Monday morning wife, weeping
  behind the sunglasses of her shame,
Truth about the insecurities of the man to blame,
Truth about the cities, the scabs that adorn
  the face of earth like weeping sores
  on the whore that was born of money,
Truth I found in a forest full of circles, where
  birth is death and there is no shame in trees
  that reach for the sun in a sky devoid of dogma,
  in streams that know where to go
  and laugh all the way to a bank of earth,
Truth I heard in the first nation's drums,

Drums that propel fancy dancers in glorious circles
  in the northern forest, the open plains,
In Africa where there are not enough dollars for mercy.
In Alaska where Inuit igloos reverberate with
  the throb of drills, seeking dinosaurs,
In Detroit and Chicago, where the drums circle round
  guitars that weep for lost circles,
In Katmandu, where unanswered prayers flap
  on warmer winds and snow melts in nuclear winter,
In Denver, where poets remember Jack's Buddha
  in multi-syllabic maps to simpler paths
  where even gods find peace in circles.

A poet's rhymes should raise the reader's eye to stars.
Words must try, at times to shine like those
  diamonds, glittering in the vast mystery.
The hands of a poet must not grasp at weapons
  but tend the gardens of the mind as if to
  hold the weight of holy breast in gentler grip
  and drip phrases with the rhythm of
  waterfalls to salve the wounds
  and lead the way, all the way, home.

odious ravens wait

   in quazi-spiritual
control modules

with altar-boy dipsticks

    ironic, like
ribald nuns or

the putrefaction of
   expired angels

this is the export
   of ochre missionaries

with bullets, languages
   and gods

hebrews know god too
   with six-million excuses
for terrorism

as muslims prey with
   AK-47s
kali wears her
   belt of hands

even lao tzu was a
   military strategist

gods weep as they are loaded
   into the breeches
of guns

as the last egg

breaks

The author of my fury is war
and handmaidens of waste and greed
light a furnace for my children.

Urbanians penetrate the forest
in large vehicles -
penetrate
the greatest lake
in phallic boats
devoid of paddle or wood.

I seethe at the hunger for innocent souls
to join a nation of misunderstood gods
in cannibalistic cabals that
call bombs patriot.

The fires of commerce consume
aboriginal wisdom with teeth
mislabeled Jesus, mix the ashes
of the dead languages of actual earth
in concrete cauldrons of
fictional history to fill
libraries and graves.

Asphalt lakes lap at shores of maize
to fuel the fires named progress
and the smoke rises from the grave
of understanding.

Blue phrases erupt from open eyes
that see tomorrow die
in the abattoir of broken bodies
contained in cement boxes
at the end of inferno.

The sun, herself
will consume the consumers
who know nothing of circles
as my own blue circle
grows cinders.

A grey stone circled a blue
stone circled the sacred fire
and actual God knew momentum
The oceans knew the tides
imposed by sister moon
and a salamander oozed
into gravity

He shed the need for balance
and grew arms to gather,
a long stride to patrol
boundaries
His need to mate was paramount
and led to dancing, to mirrors
where he found gods
and false fire

He obscured the sun with steeples
and invented clocks to govern
slaves to his false fire
and bombs, bursting in air
to roast lemmings

The artist, the poet, remembered
circles but potentates ate them
with lithium and wars
The singers of the one sun still
sang from mountain and forest
but the guns spoke louder
than the flower

At last the gasoline burned
the skin on azure earth, the
oceans grew, the sky burned
with seething rainbows
and the circle closed

After the time escaped from clocks,
grew round, and round again
a floating cell grew legs
and swam for smaller
shores

I got off the long dog in Memphis, had to score, get
well and besides, there was blues and ribs.
There was a guy in the bar at the second beam, a
twenty bag, and DAMN!, that city junk hit har…
Nodding a bit in the stall and Big Somebody, or
Fat Somebody, or Son Someone shakin'
the wall with my desperation
and the ghosts.
Mr. Gibson was singin' sweet.
Mr. Beam listened to broken dreams and
I got a little boy an' girl, got into the women's room
with the blonde with the spinning odometer.
Dirty knees, good times, a fix, but jus' chippin'
really.
The big dude in the corner with all the
bowling shirt guys was her husband, I guess,
because my damn ears were bleedin' my
knuckles were broken again, my
buzz was gone and John Law was in the
house.
I must've mentioned inbreeding or somethin'
'cause the nightsticks made me piss blood
for a week to remind me I'm not funny.
Now I'm down, in Memphis
with a monkey on my back and 120 days
for my works and a bad sense
of humor.
Viet Nam didn't have nuthin'

on Memphis…

She leaves trails on my mind
like Owsley Sid or earthworms, after
another loud knight of rain
or pain, trails like guilty stains
on the white cotton of morning's
cloud.

She makes me creep across the night
like those earthworms
in search of writhing, knowingly cashing
another emotional rubber check
in that supermarket where she scours
the aisles for momma, and love
has callused hands.

When her pen weeps
my last moon sinks into my last sea
and I am redundant,
redundant,
redundant,

but, with a wry smile and a roar
she soars above the sub-urban sprawl
with wings of salty phrase, ascendant
strides, into the realm of Carhartts
and lingerie, with a bic, an attitude,

and magic.

It was poetry that killed us after all;
the language that spawned our discontent.
Was the intellect that separated us merely fate?
Was ego a God's ironic suicide?
Was this that one black thing
that Sylvia and Anne understood?
That they breathed?
The sun consumed the eyes of the
brightest dinosaur.
That first mathematician, call him
Necromancer, counted stones.
The machinations of man usurped the
sacred circles to form wheels.
Philosophy was birthed to craft excuses
As apes found mirrors in new ponds
and Gods in new mirrors.
Columns of fabricated numbers divided
building blocks to illuminate the garden
and a million Hiroshimas bloomed
like suns of a father who eschewed
other Gods.
Blame Sam for these dark verses
as it is his Albatross that pecks them
from my throat.
I need to drive my wheels sixty words
of distance to read radio poems and
a man with some other God insulted an
idiot's father so mispronounced
speeches killed brown men and tin
soldiers so I can burn dinosaurs and
a capitol W can smirk.
Curse Allen for making me howl, for
using this bloody tool to magnify
the whole in the dike.
We use our X to magnify ourselves
until no blue stone may hold us because
we see nothing beyond the next big O.
The nations of beast, of bird, of butterfly,
all lost to the cost of our sentience, as
two words prevail – the end…

If I be mouse, my
cheese be nothing, my
sunlit field, invisible.

My twitching nose, my whiskers -
but dreams of rodentia.

My mate's eight fine teats
are only distractions
from nothing -
from all.

If I be man, my
bowl be empty of stew
or opinion that grew
from many things
to obscure
nothing.

For nothing is everything
after all, like a
circle

waiting

for everything…

Even the bearded poet, or Jack's
   pimp in a long red car is
   magnetized as willow
   to divine the next wet
   Xanadu.

As my lofty adjectives eat open
   microphones and the sax bleats
   the beat of first moans, it is
   mons that defines this quest.

Forked tongues, like forked stick
   or romantic metaphor are but
   tumescent tongues, prodding
   at the only grail a man
   can sing.

From that well, that moistened
   church, emanates the whisper
   of the moon, the warm base
   of the only actual rainbow.

My compass pen, my steady north,
   defined by a magic triangle,
   yanks my branches into
   dances, irrevocably drawn

     into the void of Freud.

I want to go to New York in the spring
and sell poems.
I think it's because of the falcons
that roost on the ledges and make
them write about rivers they never fished
or women they never fucked.
I want to sell poems to soft men that smell good
and think Thunderbird is an automobile.
I want to write pages with cheap wine, ashes
and barley, print them in real books.
I'm all I've got so I'll write about flat mahogany
and two AM sluts, wobbling to a smelly room
with droopy eyes and low self-esteem.

Let the tweedy gents with too many opinions
carve out the stains while I seduce the fat receptionist.
Let the teachers preach about Haiku and wave
collegiate stop signs at inner city adjectives; they
build their own sterile ghettoes.
I will not write about those two nails I pounded
in 1972 as the voice of blue-collar America
or those elysian fields I never saw, but the
wine and cheese reading, where I pounded the wine,
puked on the blond, and tried to read "Howl".
I will fling my I's like slinging guns in a
black confessional, like screams from my asylum.

That junior editor in New York that expected a
poet to sit on the front stoop, rumpled, with
a brown paper bottle and a notebook full
of midnight holes punched in walls and
the traditions of Bukowski will find me

on a ledge.

As my days become finite

    volumes spill from my pen
    in a verbal epiphany of compost
    or wherewithal for philosophers
    in a future poetic renaissance
    of my imagination.

As my earth becomes finite

    I see Texans in pickemup trucks
    full of currency tipping a blue
    marble on a right-canted axis
    with silicone-breasted cheerleaders
    chanting for paunchy potentates
    late, late in the autumn of man.

As my love becomes finite

    and gravity has its way with ladylove
    who winks with crows feet and wings
    the man in the mirror finds my sin
    and my mouth emits,
    "Why, I remember when…"
    while sunflowers bloom on pupils
    that see new menus for old dinosaurs

    I see redemption
    in her starlit eyes.

As my proximity to enlightenment
    becomes finite

    the moon mocks my magic
    with blue orbits in a thicker sky
    that forgot my songs as a pincushion
    for smokestacks, a conduit
    for a parade of ones and zeros

that proclaim everything in the world 156
and the dirty-pretty pomes that live
where language went to the
elephant's graveyard of thought
and illuminated the void
that Walt once filled
to clutter small computers.

As my stanzas become finite

my ghost-poem reveals its breasts
but never the warm whole of itself and
there is a swarthy monument to ferocity
eating my mouth at microphones
and poetry readings to hurl invective
at capitalists, neocons, and other
scavengers, as if to scream in Braille
for blind sheep, but he finds pomes
in clear streams.

Focus

From sun and moon
star and womb, we exit into
a world with a focus for
each eye, inner, and outer
    It is not moot that this
temple be crowned
by erectile tissue
with many magicians
inside.

When the fog from the east eats the
islands, it's as if a metaphysical monster in some
distant land had whispered a dark

secret, but

still

the blue creature, wrenching at my
id like some frigid tormenter may mirror itself
in an unseen lake like
colder fire,

but still

a poets monster may yet relent and let the
blue hounds sniff at some other carcass today, let
the spectacle play out like dry ice
in a galvanized bucket, yet

the years are a grayer blue now, the singing

distant, the Gods more quiet, more

still

as the morning sees me, the sun never burns the
distant breath of lost dreams from clouded eyes
or sins from a tired poet gone cold in
an invisible lake.

When it snows this hard in march, it's as if
some grandma is riding a dildo.
There is no beauty in it.
The time is past and it seems to come down gray.
The truck is buried again and I'm over that shit.
This flask fits my hand better than the shovel
and I'll git that sumbitch out come spring.
It's time to write another poem with amber ink.
Time to spark up a doob and lube my imagination –
to forsake the nation of Babylon, cast aside my mask -
to drain the flask and bask in the muse of Bourbon -
to light a poetic fuse that imbues my phrases
with irreverent wit in fits of imagined grace –
and thus to flow like some drunken dervish.

When it snows this hard in march, on frozen
mud and false rumors of flowers, I raise amphetamine
eyes to leaden skies and clench a pen to write
my way to other skies that hold a wealth of rain.
The Bourbon put television windows in the
kitchen and brookies in the crick that
thawed behind the shed.

I see the children, small again, out in the yard, playing
with newborn chicks that chirp the song of June.
I see her, in the garden, weeding topless in july
and innocent in her beauty when she still loved me.
I see the Geese of all those orange autumns, pointing
the way to freedom.
I see a man, bent by time and stiff of joint, on the
porch, rocking to the very beat of tides while
counting syllables for sublime sonnets.
In the bliss of Bourbon sunsets.

I see that it is time to refill the flask…

Since the diagnosis, I understand Edgar better.
The ghosts swell inside to ride my pen.
Guilt is immortal, shame, a vigilant master.
My fist, my tongue's cruelest lash, created
shadows that catch me as I weaken in
the grip of time and conscience.

Like demons of my own device, they lurk
in my mirror, my excuse, my Karmic burden.
Where are my legs to stand as grandfather or
man, when they take the breath to name me such?
Such dingy recompense, the voices that
name me sinner as I earn the sound.

There is irony on the road to my good night.
As straighter roads prevail on purer map, the
detours and alleys of other days populate
my dreams with screams that tear the
night with verses of mayhem, visions
of ravens I painted on the canvass of my life.

I wear my heart on a black leather sleeve,
and my ghosts in a faraway gaze.

"Didja hear?

Jaime came back, all fucked up."
"Rob, man, when your time comes, you
get your ass to Canada, ain't nothing
but death over there."
"They say the babies 'r' all fucked up
from the orange; shit man, they
fogged us with it for three
days on that goddamn hill."
"The leg and the hand ain't no
thing man, a ticket to the world"

"You goin' to the courthouse today?"
"Yeah man, gonna burn that
Motherfucker right on the steps;
ON TV!"

Now I only see them in parades, all
out of place, with wheelchairs, peace
symbols, cammies, and that
thousand yard stare
in a gray haired and proud
company of patriots
and beneath the overpass
in the cardboard squalor
of lost heroes and
blown-up saints
that mumble inconsolable
dreams on the breath of
a glass thunderbird;

invisible.

There is a box in my head
with god and everything in it.

On the face of a blue world
men pry at themselves with
gods, hungry for names and blood.

With swords and napalm, they preach
to pagans of peace and commerce,
growing maps, multiple births that
deny the sacred shape of womb,
and a violent collective box, but
these are not my boxes, that
judge the tribes with guns
and angry prophets.

These are not my boxes, that
flail at the breasts of mothers
with propaganda that makes demands
with angry faces like the one
in a pastor's mirror, faces
in temples and mosques that
reflect their builders faces,
faces that hunger for war to
fill collection plates with the
glory of their faces.

I was drowned in the water
that filled my little box until
a little god wanted me to die
in the killing of yellow men
with another box.

Outside that box, I could breathe.

My own box began to grow from other
waters, from drums, from churches
in the sun, that needn't name my
box, or define my love for it, from
actual rivers that sang actual psalms.

I could not open it, but dancing
made holes in it, to drain anger,
judgement, and assurance.

I could not open the box
if my face was inside, or
expectations of subservience.

I could not open a box that tore
open the boxes of slaves and nations
to fill them with pale glory at
Wounded Knee and dunked them
with hoses at Selma.

Lao Tzu leaked from my box
with martial inclinations, like
Machiavelli, and other usurpers
as the years obscure the key, yet
the box fills, with children's
laughter, germination, and corn.

It fills with hope that the gods
that poison the blue circle
with greed and avalanches of
procreation will relent, and rain
will fall clear again, to anoint
upturned faces with honest waters.

I still can't open that box, but
sometimes, late at night, I see
light escaping from it.

Perhaps, it contains
the sun.

wrangle punctuation into corrals
of dissonant stanzas in mimicry of
rainbows in a wasteland of grimy slush.

Like ill-fitting pieces in some metaphysical
puzzle or harbingers of geographical fissures -
devoid of map or yellow brick poem to form
butterflies or hopeful tomorrows, they paint
grainy pictures of Anne's garage.

Miss-matched and childless, they shuffle like
blind insects on the purest parchment, sterile
masturbations of impotent rage against
libraries and merchant's blinders.

Oh, they sing, these untidy nouns and verbs,
these adjectives that adorn a Rorschach of
self-absorbed blots like lost heroes or
upside-down bats.

But these words will not dance to the tune
of retarded glee, the muffled voices of buried-head
ostriches in a sand of shifting delirium, dance
to rhythms of poisoned tides.

Where has MY rainbow gone?

dancing through my sleeping eyes
like a slippery ballet
of swans and Amazon warriors
that clench me tight
to moonbeams

Sometimes, I feel like a tampon
that may absorb mystery
but author only spurting
and innuendo

The moon is a grand merry-
go-round, and I
a grinning child
reaching forever
for a brass ring

I've grown roots to gain purchase
on the spinning breast of earth
to find the chewy treat
at the center of
myself

But still, in the waning of time
I measure myself as series of visits
to the center of

her

But I did fish the Flambeau. The
baitshop dude said cut sucker, but
I thought shrimp, so the IGA sold seafood
and bourbon to smoky fishermen.

That one trail by that bend got us
stuck by a sandbar that already had forked
sticks to advertise catfish, so the river
tasted sushi.

The big channels liked sucker meat
so the munchies steamed shrimp in tiny
circles round the green lantern.
One of the boys chummed with
bourbon and shrimp.

We all laughed in our sleeveless flannel
shirts and innocent summer night.
Three walleye fishing tourists floated by
in Birkenstocks and new kaki.
Apparently, they were not Pink Floyd
Fans.

Summer is good on the river.

in that place where the ripples go
    when a tear falls
        on tranquil waters,

to finger-paint with words for
    eyes that drink a phrase
        like a thirsty soul.

I want to wage peace in a flood
    of war, take up a verbose
        gauntlet and howl,

howl, so the very moon must
    sweep the sky with a round
        blue amen in cobalt night,

to harmonize with gentle bards
    in psalms of meek intent
        to pierce the heart of greed,

and thus to feed the mind of man
    with banquets of wise leaves
        in a blooming library
            of hope,

or get a pushcart nomination.

Ice Storm In Green

The fierce wind frolics across the forest
and the clamor of crystal castanets
rattles through the night.

Sheets of rowdy rain fall to form
emerald instruments on pine fingers.

when I piss, and now I have to tell my woman.
I'm only a man, and a poet at that, so when the flask
rustles in empty pockets, my thirst for approbation
leads me to verbose taverns, to sweaty angels.

It burns when I need to tell her that I fouled her
magic garden, that sweet home of my redemption.
It burns when happenstance casts me villain
of my drunken poems, slave to bourbon, to whore.
It burns when I piss on my mirror.

Pretentious Winter Chain

dead bonsai
frozen in blue etched soil
remembers needles

roses are not red
clocks forget the summer
blue teeth wear winter

koi jewels sparkle
a crystal picture holds
watercress and fish

{for Jackson Pollock}

Oh, Jack, dear madman, where are you?
I remember how you raped my eyes, spewing
paint on my Methodist perceptions.

Where does your image reside?

After you browbeat colors into my Jung eyes, and
you dribbled your male menses onto the
depth, the mystery of me

with the caress of magic sand through small
hourglass, I hunger yet for your manual arts.

That dancing flame still gnaws at the womb,
the mother of my quill, and moans.

And after you painted it black, on the spring
overpass, it all dimmed, privy to ghostly minions
prying at my rusty tears.

Oh, voices!
dancing on woebegone winds, Oh Sylvia,
Anne, Zelda, Hunter, Oh, Jackson, oh hope

where have you all gone?

Like vinegar, my face leaks bitter reflections
and like the town in New York, the season
takes on coppery odors, as jazz
in dingy basements

that I hide deep in poems.

Oh, drink that sponsored mayhem on canvass,
on cement and hot steel, on music, on my mirror,
I raise you high,

"A toast!", I screech, in irreverent draught of death,

     "To The Ghosts!"

Lest the poet fail to carve his words
   on the crumble of great skyscrapers
   or the deafening din of sibilant libraries,
lest he mumble incoherent lullabies
   into babes, shorn of innocent hopes
   and placate sterile editors,
lest the minstrel fail to remember
   whispers and shouts, weeping, and
   thus forget to HOWL, must he
pontificate.

SHOUT!

Shout about burning dinosaurs, poisoning
   the very breath of God,
 Shout about God, emerging from wealthy
   mirrors to throw children into
   Moloch fires,
Shout about commerce, choking the good
   earth with Mc-Styrofoam and
   rumors of sunny weapons,
Shout about the iron horses, the horsemen
   stampeding across hungry asphalt
   on the roads to nowhere,
Shout universal truths into shrink-wrapped
   Minds,
Shout kindness words to potentates,
Shout gentle Jesus to dark pulpits
   that judge mothers,
Shout, with callused fingers tapping, wrapping
   ebullient rainbows into text for academics
   to trap in scholarly volumes while
   poets seduce undergrads with low
   self-esteem.

And by these bulbous proclamations purge
   the words of pasteurized pabulum, urge
   the microphones at midnight mics
   to see the circles again, to surge to
   higher heights, to merge the
   tribes in one bright peace ~
   to paint rainbows in children's eyes,
   and whisper.

Whisper of the Lotus, weeping in false sun,
   yet bound to beauty by softest hope,
   the Lotus that bows, but will not cease
   to bloom, as even flowers must dance,

Whisper of the homeless child, that would
   exist where science elongates
   greedy merchants and feeds
   them tidy immortality,
   the child who would to feel barefoot barnyards
   but only knows the concrete beneath the
   viaduct where mercy has not met
   his sacred mother,

Whisper from poet to poet, the rhymes of
   tides, the breath of prayers in high Tibet,
   the metre of angel songs and psalms
   of peaceful midwives.

Whisper to soft leaders, the hard truth, the
   consonants of accumulated misery, the
   verbs to direct them home,

Whisper to the breeders, that immortality
   is not built of mathematics, but dreams,
   that rainbow roots live in circles that
   describe themselves to open eyes,
   and wise words may live forever,

Whisper to the crusaders, that war is a failure,
   that kindness begets strength and putrefying
   heroes honor no man.

No man may find riches in a dying blue stone.
No man may create actual gods in false mirrors.
No man knows the earth without roots.
Man is moot without tender treatment of his
    womb, his home, his good earth, good
    wife, his own good grace, his fellows.

They need whisper, our pens, of moonbeams
    and miracles, forgiveness and nouns
    like land, like wholesome meals
    for hungry generations,
    lest we lose our way,
    lest we forsake true ink,
    lest we fail to honor the ear,
    and masturbate language into
    sterile hemispheres,
    lest we stumble from
    a poet's true path,

    lest we are forgotten.

Rain in Sudan

Hope is that gentle mistress
that eases our way, devoid of war
or demand, coin or property

It will only paint itself on open eye
only thrive in diagrams of love
like concentric ripples
on clearer waters

or rain in Sudan…

We were holy in our innocence.
Barefoot, vulnerable, singing dreams
for broken boys and so we marched
on the shining palace of
broken Gods.

There was thunder in our flowers
blooming across an actual America
like smiling minstrels with peaceful
poems and redemption in beards of
guerilla poets.

We forsook napalm and burnt orange
mushrooms, blooming Pandora gifts on
poor islands, eschewed camouflage
warlords, singing marching songs to
trusting youth.

Like pavilions of brighter rainbows
our spirits shone with nobler quest.
As would children with open arms,
seek a fond embrace, we plead, all we
were asking is give peace a chance.

And now as monsters stalk again, the
flower-folk must rise again, to march
on ivory towers in protest of genocide
in distant lands, of greedy expenditure
of patriots for prophets.

The amber glass, the smoke
should mix Hemmingway's
nads with Corso's crazy-cool
genius, even Sexton's weeping
ovaries on this dull page

and sage proclamations ensue
to the rue of poets and pig-fat
seasoned with saffron and thickened
with flour and anecdote

but the machine is filled with
the blond, the blond, the blond
in the corner with crinkled
erectile tissues issuing forth from
behind a skimpy top and
muse in her ample hips

swaying to songs I don't know
but would be happy to write
badly for her.

Settling for infernal rhyme, for
clumsy metaphor to open the poem's
door and spill light into a burning
world, wrestle Herculean monoliths
onto tablets of a stoned troubadour
in four, four, four ababab is not

in this glass, the fuse of confusion has
been lit in a fit of pseudo-abstract
ramblings in a cloud of illegal
blue, wafting into the
first rain in ages

and two run-
on sentences.

I love you nude in the garden
and the dew that moistens my poems.
The sweet gravity of pear that seeks my palm
with the thunder of secret rhythms behind.

I love red wine on alabaster, nectar on a bloom
and the marching of shudders on supine slopes,
the texture of raisins from love's deft touch,
and the murmer of wind through quaking limb.

I love the tide when beach and water are one
and the picnic feeds writhing souls robust flood
in the pulsing of twined vines and burst fruit.
The gate opens to private acres of precious ache.

I love the flavor of blueberry abstracts, consumed
by a muscular serpent, given to spilled words
and pontification of downy grail. The plunge
into the very mystery of you. The harvest.

Psssssst,
c'mere, the Siren implored, not
the Midwest tornado or someone crashed
one, but she, emerging…
Dali's metronome bent a moment into days
and cycles of the infinite monotone, gray tones of
merging liquid to solid to spirit.
She spoke of tides, known by the first
nations of men, of many circles, sang months
and minutes of songs like dolphins sing
without notes or words, but auditory dances with god.
She explained that man is not matter, but intention,
not merely flesh, but fable. That bare feet connect
us to god, and god gives us many fat meals.
The wounded Albatross is a beacon, a breadcrumb
on the righteous path. This place where the blood
of earth weeps on sand and man begins
and sin was born, this solstice would mold him.
But later, up the beach, he knew she was only
the seashore, the kelp, and the mescaline.

There is no humility
In a flower, open
To the sun, rooted
To earth,
No need

But the strongest wolf is he
That shows a belly
To teeth of war,
That need only hunt,
That knows

Here is my belly
In stanzas that creep
From me
As years replace answers
With infinite
Questions

Here are my teeth
That gnash at
Distant warlords, bankers
That eat the farms
With false teeth
And infinite greed

Here I am
In the garden

afraid

I scribble pomes like Jack's pimp in a
long red car.
My haiku raised Poe's greasy birds, pecking
at my eyes like armed librarians or
scholars, marching in lockstep and the
banner reads, "SHOW, DON'T TELL!"
in quotes, attributed to a long-dead
lady with forty-three cats
and no imagination.

They remember the humor, subtle, with
slit eyes and Shinto tongues
in natures voice.
Not in actual America though, as cat lady and the
pimple-faced post-grad in the MFA program
in Timbuc Three Community Collage
have no sense of said humor.
Oh, no!

They will flay you like a thanksgiving
turkey, politely, in seventeen German
syllables, and hard consonants pecking
at eyes that see beyond
restrictions.

These tweedy gents and non-orgasmic matrons
forgot the wellspring of good American
Haiku was the glove box of that
long red car.

I think they forgot that Haiku really
don't fit this bulbous language, even when
reverently whispered through a cat
ladies whiskers, or pilloried on the steps
of the English lit dept. of Timbuc-Three
Community College, [a trailer], or
snidely rejected from inclusion in

"Floating Lilly, the Literary Journal of
Timbuc-Three Community College".

[with a circulation of seventy-one copies]

Sometimes, I get to read their little poems.

They pry the magic from poetry with
odes to rivers they never fished, flowers
they never saw from gray windows, and
love they never made.
I heard one of them actually went outdoors
once, but I never saw it.

They scorn adjectives, expletives, and refrences to
male genitals, as if each image must be
pried out of a puckered ass, tight
as a metaphor in church or the
magic beneath a little plaid skirt.

They write about nature.

Not about thick menses on a poet's lips or
the wealth of chicken shit on a well fed garden, not
about wiggly threesomes in the mud during
the first warm rain of the season, or the voice
of a bourbon-bound poet on a Harley, not
in rambling sentences with rich soil
on dirty American soles, but of
Hibiscus blossoms, never seen, watered
by tears of god that wet them not at
the seat in front of the undertaker's underwood.

Sometimes, they actually embrace non-haiku
as long as it comes from a famous perfesser, who
writes tongue in cheek verses about the
real America that he watches from the window
and calluses he never raised, but free from
adjectives or oral sex,

Like Billy Collins.

As the hill is crested
and a brother's son is lost to forever
a million sapphires gleam
to mock the tears of mourning.

When the sharp teeth of winter
bites the shore with gems, and facets
glint on waves of grief, reach to
shores of infinity, we weep.

When young flames dwindle
in other lands, beyond the ken of ice,
what splints may a poet paint
to heal the bones of grief?

The brittle sun mocks, so lovely
and devoid of warmth, it paints vistas
of blue on upturned faces, blind to
invisible miracles.

What use, a poet, without a map
to build a bridge to hope or tomorrow
when young flowers freeze?

What salve may insulate a soul
from the unthinkable, or melt an icy
fortress that holds youth beneath
a granite stone when winter
eats our young?

I will forsake words on this night
to play lilting notes to a sky full
of diamonds with a flute that weeps
like a distant loon

because he always loved
to dance.

The trails behind the fireflies
are shorter now and
the years; the evenings,
warmer.
The symphony melds from
flute to loon, to
wolf to coyotes, mimics, like
drunken fools at
karaoke in nylon
shirts.

There are ribs left, bourbon,
cicadas, sweat and moonlight
on womanflesh.
Swallows from the hayloft
fly through the eve to
feast on vampires
as the existential owl
asks who but
never why.

Poems are traded like pearls
before the swine that
rosemary graced with
prickly taste and
whisky lubricates verses
and lovers that know
the songs the wolves
sing to the moon.

She was a soiled angel in an asphalt hell, this
   Grace, and her eyes,
   broken and chipped by concrete years,
   still reflected sun.
Her days wore condoms full of chronic
   desperation and broken syringes
   in the gutters of Babylon, but her
   spirit wore ballet slippers.
She walked like a sonnet on Plath's hot
   path, but her hips swayed like the delta.
Perhaps, it was daddy that set her on this path,
           {she never said}
but something dismal led her to this shadowed
   place, where hope is a dream that haunts.
Grace was invisible to commuters and other
   miscreants, but the poet saw her shining
   like new money in a beggar's hand, or
   rain to end the pain of drought.
His eyes were gluttons for leaves of sages,
   pages of wages of men who danced on paper
   with electric bodies on paths less traveled,
   by men with a taste for ravens and
   nightmares with an albatross,
   and his heart was a home for wounded doves.
When calamity meets muse in shades of gray,
   night meets day in incongruous rainbows,
   like a ray of light on Pollock's overpass
   or a poem on a bar-napkin.
And now, today, when his words play as if
   to fill the mouths of ancients yet to come,
   and stories of hope unfold in the folds
   of a gentler brain and spill to the leaves
   of autumns hence, it is all because
   he was saved by Grace.

I saw the grim reaper
dressed in institutional white.
I saw the war machine
hungry for farm boys
and steel.
I saw a daughter meet
my hands at the precipice
of extinction, heard her
sister caterwaul from
the dumpster
of youth and sanity.
I saw a slain king, a dark
emperor, and skies the hue
of a bruise on a servile
back.
I watched the death throes
of freedom when the
chimp put the fox
in the henhouse.
I saw a needle prick my soul
with ecstasy and doom.
I saw an albatross foresee
this greasy Halloween
from leaves, floating
in the library
and I wept.
I looked in the mirror
and beheld my questions
where others find god.
In the salt of feminine oceans
I heard drums and hope
but the cannons are
louder than the moon
and blue tone
prevailed.
I looked into the heart of man
and screamed.

when glum is my secret name
     and hoof-beats reverberate
My tempting sister
      carries hope in a rainbow purse

She sees stars with eyes that weep diamonds-
      sings me sunsets at midnight

If irreplaceable could shine as a prince
     and time wear two vestments
the very sky would sing to the
     writhing of poets

If a river could fathom her
     it would delight at hard stones
that help it's clarity climb
     over landscapes of time

She is the salve for our mortal dark-
     the light that saves morning
from mourning, from ochre
     enclaves, from selfish fears

She is light, and we, the tanned

bask in her sweet song.

" I write a lot of mediocre poems,
    but the good ones write me,"
    -- Rob Ganson

Writing Poems in the Snow

It's snowing, and snowing.
All the poems turn to slush, as
I wonder when I need to plow
again.
I try to write of multicolored grandmothers-
dancing, in the earthen church
of a new and hopeful society, and
a necromancer, spending young men,
but my eye measures the drought-breaking
prisms, catching the sun, in the breath
of all the gods

and all I can wrap my pen around
is the new old truck, the boss plow, and
one hundred and five thousand miles,
one hundred and five dollars worth of gas
in the maw of that V-8 beast, so I can
get out for smokes, when I fall off
the wagon again, and to read
radio poems Thursday, about
saving the environment.

Snow is ironic.

Oh, I strap on the flask of a metaphorical
St. Bernard, and coax some phrases free,
I even rhyme occasionally, wearing off
my fingerprints, sonneteering, in the
mood for well-formed vanity,

but, with an illegal grin, again and again,
my muse makes snow angels, to
trip me in the dark grip
of pragmatism.

Blessed is the Saxophone player
that can riff with the turn of phrase

Blessed is the soldier that lays down guns
to embrace a child with actual arms

Blessed are those who find god
in the sun, the moon,
the crops she supplies
but never in a mirror or a bloody crusade

Blessed are the judged, not the judges

Blessed is the drummer, that plays
the heartbeat of tides for innocent feet

Blessed is the warrior for peace, who
hurls flowers and hope through a bullhorn
to illuminate the antichrist in a white house

Blessed is the grandmother, daughter of
the moon, and keeper of patience, who
knows the way home

Blessed are those who give god no name,
no dogma, but live nearby

Blessed is the man who knows nothing
for he may learn all

Blessed is the gardener, who grows
strong daughters, beautiful sons,
and maize

Blessed is the general, who leads
from the front, in defense of innocents
but never for maps or commerce

Blessed is the teacher, who learns everything
in the eyes of a child

Blessed is the poet, who plants
plump seeds of truth in the
open minds of the hungry

Blessed are the strong, unafraid
to appear weak

Blessed is the man who seeks himself
for a lifetime, and finds himself

wanting

The Christmas in my Mind

HO times three and my mind
lies on a beach, with umbrella drinks
and an Elvin lass

 in butt-floss.

From Stockton's shore to barren's floor
blue orbs glisten in northern light
With yeast adorned and sweet juice
filled, they hide in emerald home

In bygone age they graced the taste
of pemmican, with mingled fat
They filled the bear that filled
the night with mystery

From sandy glen, they fill abstract
pancakes with azure treasure
A country kitchen dances to the
aural symphony of baking pies

 As time knows the north, the berry;
the gather-men push higher
The SUV and Mc Tourist wave
washes upon Superior shore

Wine, for the green visitor, propellant
for plastic kayak, for sustainable
standard of consumptive culture
and a quart to take back to gray city

But away from the bustle of urban
influx in the real country, the cabin
in the forest, blue giggles adorn
the grandchildren of summer,

barefoot still

I received an email from a gifted poet that
wrote a story about a hooker and a cello as
well as letters to Squeaky Fromme.

Kurt was dead.

I stopped writing about rivers I never fished
{like the Susquehanna} with pre-requisite
humor like the dimmest laureate, to write about
REALITY in surreal solidarity like Mr. Vonnegut.

I pondered on the tendency of genius to extinguish
itself like the Gonzo gun I heard on public radio
or Jim's romantic Paris, or Kurt's non-exit in the
year of Orwell's prediction.

The bleating of sheep that keep repeating the
anointing of greasy lowest common denominator
to lead us to wars, and, wars, and wars, and crusades
and crusades, and four-wheel drive city asphalt
vehicles, and country-and-western music, and
boy bands, and hip-hop buffoonery is all so damn
heavy as Gods found in lying mirrors hurl bombs
and furious invective.

The retarded man that masturbates a Viagra-erected
mini-prick in a circle of sycophants and toy soldiers
insists that torture is only torture when practiced by
non-Amerikans while his handlers hope the aware
will see him as the disease and not just a symptom.

He has a God in a mirror and his ear, and despite the
echo he hears his instructions to glorify God with foul
deeds; to heed the call to lead from the rear and stalk
the airwaves with the idea that we must protect our
terrorists from the other terrorists where they aren't
until they are.
Things are simpler now that Saudi-Arabia has annexed
Texas.
Perhaps together, they can wrestle Washington from

Israel, stop arming both sides and save me some tax
money so I can get a larger automobile and burn
more dinosaurs.
I wait for Billy Pilgrim's aliens to whisk me away from
this blissful bastion of bullshit, this state of disrepair,
this warming air, this incendiary air that gnaws at the
spirit like Mr. Rosewater's reality.

Nobody seems to notice the withdrawal of Lake superior,
the gleam from troubled waters, the air that used to be
invisible, the sun that sizzles now that the Hummers and
Escolades invade the northern lands across the bodies of
the lower-class youth that die to supply the oil for the
wealthy cancer that eats ate the shore with condos and
merchants that make nothing, build nothing, grow nothing
know nothing, save that the poor are there to serve them.

LET THEM EAT DOLLARS!
LET THEM HEAT WITH DOLLARS!

Listen to the beat of the first nation's drums.
Let us see the cat's-cradle of commerce in it's greedy mirrors.
Sing the peaceful song of the humanist.
Beat back the "ice nine" of false Gods.
Feel the breath of four holy winds.
Seal the deal by renouncing filthy green papers
that feed no man.
Plan to love the land again, praise it with vegetables.

Denial is a polluted place and by the grace of open eyes
may we yet walk greener paths, raise upturned faces to
the stars and place our trust in honest heroes, disgrace
not our children, with a legacy of doom that looms so near
but heal ourselves of greed, feed them a future
of peaceful possibility.

Mr. Vonnegut is dead and I can't write about a false
blue-collar world.

My hands are too callused to write clichéd lies from
academic niches where riches accumulate from incestuous
presses that publish pretentious pap disguised in everyman
garb and prerequisite humor. It's time to write LOUD!

Oh, pattern, rhymed to find the heart of man
Oh, Pantoum, that paints with rhythmic brush
Sing the peace of forest, of farmed land
Paint us songs of butterfly, of maiden's blush

Oh, Pantoum, that paints with rhythmic brush
Purge me of city lights, fill my eyes with green
Paint us songs of butterfly, of maiden's blush
Fill my pen with miracles my eyes have seen

Purge me of city lights, fill my eyes with green
And within the form of stanza's bright design
Fill my pen with miracles my eyes have seen
Plant rainbows in soil of opening urban minds

And within the form of stanza's bright design
Sing the peace of forest, of farmed land
Plant rainbows in soil of opening urban minds
Oh, pattern, rhymed to find the heart of man

II

That form and function follow suit
With balanced form and simple rhyme
To mingle words with gentle flute
And paint them verses, clean, sublime

With balanced form and simple rhyme
Would my pen paint the girth of earth
And paint them verses, clean, sublime
To balance the greed of men with mirth

Would my pen paint the girth of earth
To holy rhythms of tide and blue moon
To balance the greed of men with mirth
And thus, the psalms of earth to croon

To holy rhythms of of tide and blue moon
To mingle words with gentle flute
And thus, the psalms of earth to croon
That form and function follow suit

Forsake not rhyme
To songs of green
Chime in prime time
With words you mean

To songs of green
On simpler paths
With words you mean
Paint rain's soft bath

On simpler paths
On carpet of fern
Paint rain's soft bath
That peace, we earn

On carpet of fern
To songs of green
That peace, we earn
Forsake not rhyme

IIII

Peace
Land
Release
Man

Land
Heart
Man
Art

Heart
Dream
Art
Gleam

Dream
Release
Gleam
Peace

On the seventh day of the seventh month
of the seventh year of the dark millennium
the void was born in Faustian spaces
of a troubled cranium.

Kurt's exit predicted this Dresden of the soul,
this open-eye syndrome that mimics the
metronome of some vast clock that
counts the days of man.

The rotting corpse of an albatross has
eaten the daffodils, regurgitated wars and
odd kings across the social landscape
of a suicidal species.

The black smokestacks belch mc-death
as high priests bend altar boys over tables
of mathematics to enter the banks and
churches of men with god in mirrors.

I will carry this void in a tattered knapsack,
speak of it in tongues and poems to the
last humans with human ears and tears
for the children we eat,

shout to the towers of power for the return
of the hope I lost in the time of sevens,
rant with scant aplomb to high heavens
of the scars on my son's world

and demand peace!

"Farewell, farewell! But this I tell
To thee, thou Wedding-Guest
He prayeth well, who loveth well
Both man and bird and beast"

Samuel Coleridge

Torn Sheets

There are tears in the fabric
    of a mariner's sails
and the universe.

A stronger orb eats parched shores
    with skeletal smile, and
dead leaves flutter.

The cradle of civilization
    does not rock maternal, the
husband in the moon
      has forgotten the tides
    and the screech
of a dead albatross
      on a greasy shore.

Dirty sheets ripple in an ill wind
    defined by banks and warlords
dance on parched continents.

Dirty sheets ripple in the beds
    of forsaken woman
in the grasp of commerce
      and menses.

Here, on the edge of the world
    the grandmother drums
      are silent in the oraface of man
and the poets shout no more.

Will we sit, cross-legged at the

mergence of desert to
   dead sea and scribble
scrolls of mild verse and
   pre-requisite humor -

or storm the stairs of forbidding
   libraries with strong epithet
   and pens, brandished
like stronger weapons
for peace, for beasts that foul not
   our mirrors or the
churches of the open mind?

In the church of more
   would I preach the least
    to tame the beast of progress

on these coffee stained sheets.

Weight

They say the spirit
Weighs twenty-one grams
Darlin, when my time comes
Bend to me
Drink my last poem
From the lips that sculpted your
Sighs through these autumns
Drink deeply

And weigh yourself

i was running along a long, long wharf, barefoot
   of course, and the gravel

And she was sitting next to me
                            on the silver dog
feeding my artist image

Splintered shards of seas
          glistened to each side

This would be my thesis at the collage college

This image, this kaleidoscopic portent that
                 so inflamed
She, She, She, of the smile, the peasant
         dress, the smile, the protuberant

nipples was channeling MY Dali!
      Feeding him to me on
a Ritz

Far, Far yonder, at the end of the wharf, was
              My muse – in – a – box
on a guillotine
   the gleam was poised with the military
     inclinations of Lao Tzu and there
       were Christmas ribbons –
        and bows

The sky was liquid chrominum
   There were two suns, with names
      beginning with sexy whys
        that knew my real name

The scene drew my rapid feet like
    sugar–snaps on a distant
        trellis

She stirred, swirled, and I had a glimse
    down her bodice

Over a tie – dyed shoulder was no shore
 in this dance with Shikantaza
    [Dogen Kigen's simply sitting]
     No turning back
       only shards, and shards

No return ticket offered
No railing to hem me in, but only
 intermittent galvanized poles, two art-deco
   speakers to each, trailing wires-

in abeyance to lost umbilicus

She moved again and
    I caught a whiff of my ardor

Andy Warhol, that pale imp, that scavenger
    held the rope in limp grasp
      as the raven on his shoulder
       predicted dire events
"Don't you pull that rope, motherfucker!"
    I panted
"I will inflict violence!"
         But I grew more distant

Odd notes chirped from the shards to my left
   A dissected porpoise, smiling
     clutching a golden key in cubist beak

She, oh she, awoke beside me –
    kissed me deep with breath that
      reeked of sweet chaos
        and I knew that I would fuck her.

[self portrait in blue]

Never mind the man behind the curtain -
gesticulating in his verbose Oz.
His self-aggrandizing lines are certain
rhymes, bound to predictable bla, bla, blas.

He peels back flesh to show us intestines-
writhing in gloriously exposed shame
on some stoned philosophical quest in
an effort to fan some infernal flame.

Existential angst erupts from his pen
like spunk from a masturbating monkey.
He preaches for peace again and again
but he's angry and his meter's funky.

Often, he writes from way out on a limb
waiting for an audience to catch him.

Swatting Swarms of red men to open new lands with sunny sided
semantics of pacification, the sadistic salutes to new gods fueled
us as shocks surged and curtain cries of first nations reverberated
and the collared collective of black robed ravens blemished beauty
of silenced flutes with European syllables, ack-acking greedy gods
into the captivated chaos of smallpox reservations and great white
greed. Thus, we opened America to the bucking bronco of money.
The fiddling fingers and leather lashings of the south called my blue
brothers to ashen alleys of Fredericksburg, a patchwork playground
of bellowing barricades that rocked the fickle foundations of lily
white greed. The zealous zephyr of mirrored image and pious pulpit
and the wicked whining of twisted twins, merchant and fool, whipped
up the waning whirlwinds of war in Europe. War had claimed the
very sky with a cry for the absolute annihilation of men who knew
not the son of callous captains in a good book, misread by minstrels
of mayhem and our hands knew wonderful weapons to gather the
glory befitting the cerebral containment of death from afar. Fiercely
feigning the chafed chastity of the innocent, We wear the medals of
glory, of carnal calamities rendered by we, the soldiers, in the
tactical tilling of foreign soil with ever bigger bombs. I am universal
soldier. Whether the wafting winds of Hiroshima share the burnt-meat
odor with the verdant breeze of Viet Nam, or the gunsmoke in Ohio,
I will fight until the televised tribulations until the crayola canyons
of Iraq weep oil into Texas banks and Muslim dreams drain from
bulletholes as we are masturbating memories of the glorious grail
to the dim ears of public perception as we pander to the patriots who
line Pandora's box. Salute me as tremors trip the July forth skies…

Oh noble bean, of forest born, a feast
    for senses six,
        sing that earthy tone.

Of grandma's kitchen, of nook, where
    scents alone may mimic gods.

No faint adjective for plain are you, but
    grand nouns, dancing on tickling
        tongues, bound for glorious
            repast on alabaster.

Rolled on muslin, kneaded in rising dough
    or gracing that softest flesh, living
      beneath the mystery, the cloud
        of white cotton.

Songs of comfort and warmth do you sing
    as psalms of strings, plucked on
        dulcimer or stroked on lute.

And angels dance on a poet's trill at the
    harmony of heaven's flavors

when she adds the cinnamon.

Shaking, clammy, in a ten-story flop
skin, crawling with imaginary bugs,
she needs to get well, make the shaking stop.
Her crusted veins can feel the needle tug.

Head for a nickel, the works for a dime,
the bug ain't bit her yet, but give it time.

She used to be daddies little princess-
traded her pony for the horse, and less

The cheerleader waits on a sweat-stained bed
for black-tar death that shines like diamonds.
She needs the heroin to blot her head
since the night when daddy ripped her hymen.

There's a hole in her arm where the sorrow goes
but daddy's okay, cause nobody knows.

Zen and the art of muse maintenance

Pomes should not plink upon innocent
paper like verbose turds, but
titillate the page like lovers tongues
or splash it like metaphysical
menses.

This one has the impact of Smith-Corona
whacks on softest skin of dead aspen.

The masturbation of words must wring
the juice from life like the most
demanding concubine wrings
currency from limp organs,

supplicant in the green church.

Harley-Davidsons have poems in them.
Geo Metros have none.

Sex has no poems without orgasm
or violence, she can fake it, the
poet cannot.

The birth of a child in rhyming couplets
is cliché, but not the flavor of
the placenta.

Bourbon, hardship, being in love with
a slut, wars, daffodils, erections, elections,
broken bones, hearts, and promises,
as well as dingy taverns are avenues
strewn with poems,

side streets with purple palettes.

Security will not leak your actual ink
but a rusty razor will surely spill
the guttural juice of fruits
like Allen, adorn the circle
with bent languages from
trembling tongues, from
hesitant genius.

Enlightenment lies not in the poems
you write, but those that write you
and the clitoris contains the
rhythms that tides mimic

My muse flies over distant mountains
like a pock-marked saint to see
the prayers flap on high eastern
breezes on Mondays, dances
out of reach naked, trembling, moist
with ink.

A muse may only be caught barefoot.

There is wealth in poverty but the
merchant has forsaken the quill
and muse eats peanut-butter
and jelly while rich
men stutter mono-syllabic
rumors and

instructions.

Obstructions form in academic circles
as the muse dies beneath rules
written by fools with postscripts
to given names and the
shame is evident in the mediocrity
of Dick and Jane verse but my
diatribe will fill the hive of man
to subjugate curses of
pretention.

Fuck Daffodils!

My muse, after- all
has callused hands.

There are no more bees and few
trees but mindless drones extinguish
themselves in sandy banks while
politicians distinguish themselves
with the bodies of the poor and more, more,
 more.

My muse lives on the wrong side
of the tracks with the folks that pay for
wealthy heart attacks, stains on a blue dress,
and a retard bludgeoning the
constitution on the lawn
of a white house or masturbating
while he plays
with a red button and laureates
write about less than nothing.

My muse saw pyramids of naked
victims with a cheerleader
as my patriot died and they laughed
in texas and hell.

My muse read Billy Collins
and drank twenty beers
to get it.

My muse read a newspaper to inspire
funeral poems.

If I wrote one word for each
person on the planet
poetry would
be extinct.

Write a cute joke for THAT, Billy.

What if the kings got to the point,
sat down to talk about the earth,
shared a sticky organic joint,
approached our differences with mirth?

What if the brown men loved the white,
and white, with love be so inflamed
that peace be sought with all our might,
and a new dawn of peace proclaimed?

A new rainbow bloomed in oh-eight,
with a mixed palette king elected.
We must believe it's not too late
to knit the gulfs we've created.

We wait for a peaceful leader
to regenerate peace's cause
in the wake of a bottom feeder
with lucre grasped in oily claws.

What if this brown man is the one
to put ignoble gods to rest,
to join all the children of sun
in answer to his toughest test?

We mustn't feed the dogs of war
our progeny in glory's cause,
but embrace the child we adore
and pacify the bloody Shahs.

Can leaders visualize the earth
with humbler vistas of new farms
spread across our shared planet's girth
in answer to warmer alarms?

What if the year two thousand nine
is the birth of a grand new day,
the year that goals are re-defined
by kings who lay down swords to play

in the verdant fields of the lord.

About splashing through life's
puddles, not a
clever indictment
of her, a
verbous barb, aimed at her
all too gregarious genitalia,
or a made for TV movie,

not an egg-man or walrus,
certainly not macaroni,
not a viscous reminder
of last nights writhing
drying on
three sheets
to the wind,

not filler for some
ill conceived volume
of dreary reminiscence
to read at some tweedy
event with
bad refreshments
while I make eye contact with
the blond in the
corner with
low self-esteem,

but only a run-on sentence
on a Monday, bait,

trolling for that
pushcart
nomination.

(for W.S. Merwin}

The years have stampeded by
like wild horses chasing sunsets.
I hear hoof beats in shades of orange.

I remember her in varieties of blue,
emerging, beaded from the pool;
another flower, another sort of dew.

Your death killed me many times.
and it is your mausoleum, looming,
that colors my shadow so deep.

The collar on the wood cross fades
as my kaleidoscope seems to dim.
I think I've been a good boy too.

The cityscapes belch the same colors
that graced the face of my son
on the day he was never born.

Your smile illuminated a rainbow
that filled my palette of days.
My story is a portrait of you.

I drowned in your deathbed,
awash in some amniotic sea.
Revived, I can only tread water.

My mind has lost your face.
I was struck deaf when I drank
the last poem from your lips.

It's like I was born
at high velocity behind
a gravel truck, a logger

or a spider spun across
my eyes

my world is lived between
the lines
like poetry, or the view
through a Wisconsin
windshield

racing to the light

The Faces of Joy

Joy is like dewdrops on a spider web
ignited by one more dawn;
a jubilant jester, seen
in laughing children,
and daydreams

I saw it smile once in church, but
more often on the dance floor
and seldom in eyes that judge

You can find it dancing
with a child

{gazing at Andrew Wyeth's "Wolf Rivers", 1959}

Time paints a still life slowly, easing eyes
of verses from Frosty or Walt across
a canvas landscape, vistas under skies
that knew my mothers birth, her life, her loss.
It's Andrew Wyeth's brush that knew these things,
his third eye's sight that so enwraps my mind
with art's decree that men like me are kings.
He painted them in light September brings,
in the image of home that he refined.
There is a harvest of our simple lives,
even the autumn's flight of geese defined,
as are the birds, the sky, the bees, the hives,
the fields, the dreams, the cabins, the chapel,

all on display as wood grain and apples.

I wish you peace above all,
that feast of good intention
that you learn at mother's breast,
the best test of man - to that
I can attest.

I wish you clean rivers
to follow to the future,
a sea of maize to feed you.

I wish you wisdom
to forgive the weak
and know that strength
is meek.

I wish you love,
to paint your life with hope,
to spend your dance of days
at play in the fields

of nature's grand ballet.

Cause and Effect

I would live intentionally above all,
lest I blame the author of me
for some unhappy accident,

and name it god.

Lit by the flames in a fifty-five gallon drum, the black man in once green fatigues mumbles to the mad dog, with twenty-twenty vision of 1968. College hadn't been an option for a boy from the projects but the white man had a gun for him, a duty, so off he went to kill someone named Charles. Charlie killed him back, and his crumpled form was stored in the nervous hospital, full of limbless men and that thousand yard stare. After the budget cuts, they turned him loose, to mend a shattered mind on the streets of shame. Martin's dream has not yet cured his nightmares. It's mighty cold beneath that overpass.

James flips burgers on the eleven to seven shift. Some of his neighbors wear gold, drive Beemers, but that is not James's way. There is big money in Iraq, girls for the boys in uniform, medical insurance, and hope for a man willing to kill for it. The army wants James. A new black president wants James. James will come home with medals and a flag-draped box. At least they hide the boxes.

She scrubs the toilets in the governor's mansion every day. Her first son is in college, her second, in prison. He had a good job at the plant, but when the white folks quit buying those big cars, they closed. He didn't want to kill brown men for Uncle Sam, so he was serving on the corner. Twenty-five years, they say, and his babies still watch for him, come four-thirty. College loans are a lot harder to get now.

Samuel taught history at the University. After the cutbacks, the trimming, he'd been lucky to get the middle-school position. When push came to shove, the bank took his home. Ten years of equity was gone while the bank got a fat check From Dubya. He didn't expect to be back here, but at least his old car was paid for. There would be change, but would it come in time?

Ruby had a home once. When they cut off her benefits, told her she had to get a job, there weren't any. One day, at the free clinic, they took her children; "for the best, really," they said. Twenty years later, she is invisible to passers-by. They say they elected a black man, but he's just a picture on the newspapers that serve as her blanket. Ruby has a dream often. Her children are back, in Easter Clothes, searching for those eggs, in real green grass, and she wakes up weeping in thirteen sweaters. It's mighty cold on the top of the mountain.

Barack Obama is now the president, carried to office on a wave of hope. They've already spent our grandchildren's money on wars and redistributed the wealth into the largest, whitest hands until dollars are abstract slips of paper, Viagra for the top 1%. We've waged war against the Muslims for the Jews and excuse it from pews and podiums with a reminder that might makes right in this world of monsters hunting monsters hunting monsters, and we pay soldiers very well with money we don't have. There is nary a scar on Haliburton. A good man finally takes the helm of a sinking ship, tries to bribe the light to shine on a rainbow in sooty skies and my eyes alight at the sight of it. The meek have finally found a champion as the sun, itself, declares us enemies. We hope New Orleans will not be forgotten, that the torture will end, the wars; that a new color will rule in the wake of green oppression and kindness rule the day,

but, it's mighty cold
on the top of a crumbling mountain.

{10:45 AM 1/20/09}

 The first one raced in, as
the straight man for a chimp.
That imp turned the middle-class
into a urinal, and his smile
was the cake, No more rules
for the rulers, he said,
beguiling the pocketbooks
of power.

The cracker fooled them all
and so did his wife, raking in
those medical dollars
while she guaranteed nothing
by pretending to want too much.
Every time a witness tried
to testify, they shot themselves
in the eye
{from a range of twenty feet}
while they snickered at fair trade
and pacts with third-world
dictators were made.
Later, she would not campaign
in a blue dress, but regale the press
with stories about imaginary
bullets when she was put
to the test of truth.

 Oh, there were Bushes,
shading the shady Texicans,
importing Mexicans in the dark
est daze of gold fever.
Money was their Viagra, war
was their Viagra, oil was the lube,
and it was all
a Texas High School football game
until the dim one was appointed.
Out went the constitution,
the limits on contributions,
the institutions of higher learning.

The Fox was in the henhouse
and the henhouse was burning.
They called it Homeland Security
when they tapped my phone,
went fishing while New Orleans
drowned, and seeds of wrath
were sewn.

They called it interrogation
when they shamed a nation,
when they brought colonization
to the Middle East, fanned the flames
with oil and Haliburton, torture,
shock and awe, and the whole
world saw us with frightened eyes.
They called it tax relief
when they taxed the poor
to feed the rich,
fed our sons to the whore of war,
and spent our grandchildren
in their endless quest for more,
more, more.

They've poisoned our mother
beyond repair deepened
the debt ,
replaced freedom
with despair,
invaded Iraq with Blair,
and replaced freedom
with servitude from
behind the blank grin
of an idiot.
Today a new king takes the reigns
at the top of a crumbling mountain.
Perhaps freedom has been regained
in the wake of the rats,
the cracked bell will ring again
with a black man's hand
on the rope
and a new choir sing
"all we are asking..."
for the few true patriots
that remain one, in peace and hope.

Death is but the punctuation,
the end of my last stanza.,
a grand life's accumulation,
a verbose extravaganza.

I will be the dead man that spits
at kings with a great silent voice.
I'll be that burning bag of shit,
the slogan on placards they hoist.

I'll be the albatross that howls
at six oclock, on the wide screen,
fighting war with peaceful vowels
that preach to keep our mother clean.

Wherever peaceful sheep are shorn
or the meek are victims of greed,
from dusty shelves, I'll be reborn
to point at the daughters of need,

and as for god or afterlife,
never mind; read me in the park.
No The End, no period's knife,
I'll just end with a question mark

and a sigh...

Rob Ganson is a poet from the forest of Northern Wisconsin.
At home in the forest, with the stream and a garden near, his
feet are ill suited for the pavement, his philosophy, ill suited
for his occasional forays into the bustle of "civilization."

His work has appeared in numerous journals and in the
Anthologies - "Brother, My Cup" by Ea, and " Feeling is First,
Edited by Kevin Watt. His Previous collection – Float Like a
Butterfly, Sing Like a Tree, ISBN # 978-0-6151-3943-2
Is available from Long Lake Press.

Notes,

This is a work of fiction. Any resemblance to actual people or events is incendental, a part of a metaphor for a universal concept, action, or concept.

But for the natural beauty of the Chequamegon National Forest, the streams and rivers, Lake Superior, my garden, I would have little to say. Without my wife and Muse, my Donna, my children and grandchildren, I would lack inspiration and reason to preserve these messages, left to the future's children.

The following poets artists, and various other miscreants that I forget here provide inspiration, support, grounding, friendship, and some degree of objective critique. Without them, I would long since have put down the poet's pen. – Naomi Cochran, Wanda Lea Brayton, Ea, Jim Dunlop, Zayra Yves, Freak, Eric Sharp, Carol Desjarlais, Nicole, Darcy, Jeff Copenhagen, Howard Paap, Frank "Anakwad" Montano, Nicolette van der Walt, Laughing Fox, Renee, Janet Richards, Greg Alexander, Ted Gephart, Puker, Inkmaster, and Jan Chronister.

Thanks to Barack Obama for the hope. I had nearly forgotten what it felt like to smile while I voted.

Thanks to the visionary leaders of the past for the National Forests, the National parks.

After reading "Howl", by Allen Ginsberg, and the works of Walt Whitman, hearing the voice of the Zimmerman boy from Minnesota, discovering Blake, Bly, Baudelaire, Kerouac, Plath, Sexton, Ferlinghetti, Frost, Coleridge, Old Buc, all that genius, it was inevatible that my palette would be the language of the people.

I will never stop trying to revive Sam's albatross.

Thanks to Marc Creamore for his inexhaustible support, and the honor of the forward he wrote for this volume of poems.

Thanks to Dan Menzel, artist and poet extraordinaire, for his many years of friendship and creating cover art for these, my verses of hope and despair, beauty and horror, my songs of America.

www.ingramcontent.com/pod-product-compliance
Lightning Source LLC
Chambersburg PA
CBHW031952080426
42735CB00007B/358